MOUNTAINEERING IN THE
PYRENEES

25 CLASSIC MOUNTAIN ROUTES

VERTEBRATE PUBLISHING

THE AUTHOR

François Laurens was born in the Luchon Valley, where he continues to live and work. After beginning his outdoor career with the ski patrol at Superbagnères and as a walking guide, he qualified as a mountain guide in 1986. Through his work, he has climbed all the Pyrenees' most beautiful peaks, in both summer and winter, as well as most of the major summits in the Alps. He loves discovering new places and has explored many countries, far and wide. Motivated by his belief in the educational benefits of outdoor activities, he recently began working with an association that helps young people in difficulty to reintegrate into society. He is also a keen photographer whose work is frequently published in the outdoor press.

ACKNOWLEDGEMENTS

Reflecting on his long escapades in the mountains, Pyrenean explorer Henry Russell once remarked, 'It's a joy to be with someone, it's a lesson to be alone'. Therefore, I would like to express my warmest thanks to all the climbing partners who accompanied me while I was preparing this guidebook; for the wonderful times we shared and for the patience they showed in uncomplainingly posing for photographs. Thank you also to everyone who helped me put this book together and, most importantly, to my family, for their patience and encouragement.

If you would like to provide feedback on the content of this book, or if you would like me to guide you up a route, you can contact me at: www.francoislaurens.com

Cover photo: Lovely climbing on the West Ridge of Pic d'Amoulat, with superb views of Pic du Midi d'Ossau.
Back cover photo: The Troumouse Ridge.

All photography by François Laurens.

First published in 2012 by Éditions Glénat.
'Montagne-Évasion' collection edited by Pascal Sombardier.

Title of the original French edition:
Pyrénées – Les Plus Belles Courses
© 2012, Éditions Glénat, 37 rue Servan, 38008 Grenoble, France.

This English language edition first published in 2015 in the UK, Europe,
India, South Africa, Australia and New Zealand by Vertebrate Publishing.

Vertebrate Publishing
Crescent House, 228 Psalter Lane, Sheffield S11 8UT, UK.
www.v-publishing.co.uk

All trade enquiries in the UK, Europe and Commonwealth (except Canada) to:
Cordee, 11 Jacknell Road, Dodwells Bridge Industrial Estate, Hinckley, LE10 3BS, UK.
www.cordee.co.uk

Copyright © 2012, Éditions Glénat.

All rights reserved. No part of this work covered by the copyright hereon may be reproduced or used in any form or by any means – graphic, electronic, or mechanised, including photocopying, recording, taping or information storage and retrieval systems – without the written permission of the publisher, authors and editor.

ISBN: 978-1-910240-56-4

Translated from the French by Paul Henderson (traduction@paulhenderson.fr).

Designed and produced by Rod Harrison, Vertebrate Graphics Ltd,
based on an original design by Éditions Glénat. – www.v-graphics.co.uk

Printed in EU by Pulsio SARL.

MOUNTAINEERING IN THE
PYRENEES

25 CLASSIC MOUNTAIN ROUTES

François Laurens

Translated by Paul Henderson

Vertebrate Publishing, Sheffield
www.v-publishing.co.uk

CONTENTS

	Introduction & practical information	6
1	**Pic du Canigou:** Quazemi Ridge	12
2	**Pedraforca:** Traverse of the Three Peaks	14
3	**Mont Valier:** Faustin Couloir	16
4	**Pico de Aneto:** Salenques-Tempestades Ridge	20
5	**Pico de la Maladeta:** North–South Traverse	24
6	**Pic de Maupas:** West Ridge	26
	CIRQUE DU PORTILLON	28
7	**Pic des Crabioules & Pic Lézat:** Crabioules-Lézat Ridge	30
8	**Pic des Spijeoles:** South-East Ridge	34
9	**Pic des Spijeoles:** Grand Dièdre	38
10	**Pic des Gourgs Blancs:** via Pic Jean Arlaud	42
11	**Pico de Posets:** Espadas Ridge	44
12	**Pic de Néouvielle:** Trois Conseillers Ridge	48
13	**Pic de la Munia:** Troumouse Ridge	50

14	**Grand Astazou:** Oublié Couloir	54
15	**Petit Astazou:** North-West Ridge	56
16	**Pic du Marboré:** Passet Ridge	58
17	**Monte Perdido and Ordesa Valley:** Normal Route and Tour of the Valley	62
18	**Monte Perdido:** Esparrets Spur and East Ridge	66
	THE VIGNEMALE	70
19	**Vignemale:** Petit Vignemale-Pique Longue Ridge	72
20	**Petit Vignemale:** North Spur	74
21	**Vignemale:** Classic North Face Route	76
	THE BALAÏTOUS	80
22	**Balaïtous:** North-West Ridge	82
23	**Pène Sarrière:** South Ridge	84
24	**Pic d'Amoulat:** West Ridge	88
25	**Pic du Midi d'Ossau:** Traverse of the Four Peaks	92
	Huts and information	95

INTRODUCTION

'SIMPLY DIFFERENT'

'But suddenly, and as if the mountain tore itself apart, the Maladeta surged in front of us. On our left, the mountains of Auvergne, to our right, Catalonia, Spain, just there, in front of us; and we could let our imaginations run free, carrying us to Seville, to Toledo, to the Alhambra, to Cordoba, to Cadiz, scaling summits and soaring with the eagles that glide over our heads. On seeing all these jagged peaks falling and rising unequally, one behind the other, all pressed together, tightly packed and pushing to the sky, you might liken them to enormous waves in an ocean of snow that was instantly frozen.'
Gustave Flaubert

Sometimes people ask me whether I prefer the Alps or the Pyrenees. To hide my perplexity and discomfort with this strange idea of always wanting to rank everything, I generally try to get round the question by saying, 'they're just different'. Of course, there are people who adore navigating their way across glaciers, while others, but not many, relish interminable boulder fields. Similarly, some people adore the sharpness of high-altitude vistas, whereas others prefer softer, gentler landscapes. Personally, I feel that all mountains, whatever their shape or size, no matter how difficult or easy they are to climb, give off the same revitalising energy.

The Pyrenees is a 500-kilometre-long by 70- to 140-kilometre-wide chain of mountains between southern France and northern Spain. For me, the chain's most characteristic feature is its variety, as it is a veritable hodgepodge of topographies, climates and lives, jumbled together. Often it is enough to move just a few kilometres across this patchwork landscape, even from one side of a cliff to another, to find yourself plunged into a completely different environment, to imagine yourself on a new journey, transported to distant lands.

This diversity is reflected in the climbs described in these pages, which cover the entire chain from the Mediterranean coast to the edge of the Basque country. It is, of course, impossible to include every

On the Tusse de Montarqué, looking across to the Cap du Seil de la Baque.

At the start of the Salenques-Tempestades Ridge.

INTRODUCTION

quality climb in such a small guidebook, and some people may be disappointed to see their favourite route has been overlooked. However, my selection is the result of many years spent exploring every nook and cranny of the Pyrenees, combined with recommendations from other experienced mountaineers. Every route provides a wonderful day out in the mountains and will satisfy mountaineers with a taste for adventure, but each has its own unique character.

Due to the nature of the relief and changes in the climate, the list includes numerous ridge traverses but very few snow climbs. This does not mean that such climbs do not exist; however, the increasingly ephemeral nature of the snow pack means most snow and ice climbs in these southern latitudes are only in condition for short periods of the year.

In the case of rock routes, the mountains of the Pyrenees offer a very different climbing experience to that found on climbing walls or bolted crags. As a result, when choosing a route to do, it is essential to take into account a variety of factors, in addition to the technical difficulty of the climbing. Of course, technical difficulty is an important factor, but the routes described here tend to be much more demanding than their relatively low technical grades might suggest. Do not forget that most of these climbs have very little or no *in situ* gear and that climbing safely on so-called easy ground is one of the most difficult aspects of mountaineering, especially when you have to move fast.

Here, as in the Alps and all the world's mountain ranges, it is best to approach each climb with humility.

An early-morning break at the Col de Paderne.

Ibón de Marboré and Monte Perdido.

PRACTICAL INFORMATION

HOW TO USE THIS GUIDE
Each chapter begins with a summary of the following practical information:

START POINT
Brief descriptions of how to get to the huts or other start points are given in the 'Huts and information' section on page 95.

DIFFICULTY
The overall difficulty of each route is rated using French Alpine grades:

F: Easy, **PD:** Moderately difficult, **AD:** Quite difficult, **D:** Difficult, **TD:** Very difficult, **ED:** Extremely difficult.

Routes at the lower or upper end of each grade are indicated by a **+** or **-** (for example, **PD+**, **AD-**). The technical difficulty of individual sections of climbing is indicated using numerical grades from **1** to **9**. Grades up to **V** are generally expressed using Roman numerals, sometimes combined with a **+** or **-**, and grades above this level are expressed using Arabic numerals combined with an **a**, **b** or **c**. Only one or two of the routes in this guidebook include pitches harder than grade V. It is very important to remember that a route on a natural cliff may feel much more difficult than a route of the same grade on a climbing wall, especially if the rock is less than perfect, which is the case for some of the routes described here.

Some approaches are quite complex and require experience in walking on unstable and exposed ground, an exercise that is difficult to grade. The time needed to become comfortable at moving over this sort of terrain will depend on conditions, your technical ability and your fitness, but practice makes perfect. Just be patient.

TIMES
The times given are approximate and are based on a team of two fit climbers who are used to doing routes on the type of terrain described.

The Maladeta massif.

VERTICAL HEIGHT
The height difference between the start of the technical climbing and the summit. In some cases, the total height gain from the hut or car park is given.

GEAR
This section lists specific equipment needed for the route. It does not include the standard gear required for every climb, that is, harness, helmet, a few slings, accessory cord, belay device, peg hammer, a few pegs, small head torch and first-aid kit. If ice axes and crampons are needed for the route, the approach or the descent, this is indicated. Conditions can change very quickly, so ask the warden before you go up to the hut whether you are likely to need any specific gear. It is strongly recommended to use double ropes. The indications 'set of nuts' and 'set of cams' mean eight or nine nuts of various sizes, and cams from sizes 1 to 3.5, respectively. This is enough gear for most of the routes described here. Where the description indicates 'a few nuts and cams', a half set of each should suffice. 120-centimetre slings are usually long enough. It is best to use quickdraws made by tripling over 60-centimetre Dyneema slings, so they can be extended to reduce rope drag.

IN SITU GEAR
Most of the climbs included in this guidebook have very little or no *in situ* gear, so it is essential to be able to place natural protection. In addition, many pegs are very old and of doubtful solidity, so they should be tested before being trusted. It is advisable to carry a hammer with which to re-seat existing pegs. Any *in situ* gear is mentioned in the route descriptions.

PHOTO DIAGRAMS
Every chapter includes a photo, generally taken from the hut or a point on the approach, showing the general line of ascent and descent.

Line of the route:
Descent:
Dotted line indicates a hidden section.

MAPS
The French part of the Pyrenees is covered by the 1:25,000-scale IGN Top 25 maps.

The most widely used maps for the Spanish part of the Pyrenees are the Alpina series; however, these maps are of poor quality and of little use when visibility is bad. This factor should be taken into account in areas of complex topography, such as around Monte Perdido.

NAMING OF FEATURES
French names are given for summits, places and features that lie in France, and Spanish names are given for summits, places and features in Spain. Where, for example, a summit or pass lies on the border – such as the Pic du Marboré – the French name is used throughout for clarity and consistency.

Finally, training is needed in order to avoid the worst mistakes. Advice can be obtained from books, other climbers or, better still, by doing a climbing course.

PIC DU CANIGOU (2,784m)

QUAZEMI RIDGE

START POINT: Marialles Hut.
DIFFICULTY: AD. A few moves of III+, some of which are down-climbing. Some poor rock.
TIMES: 5–7 hrs in total, including 2 hrs for the ridge.
VERTICAL HEIGHT: 1,035m
CONDITIONS: as soon as the snow has melted.
GEAR: a few slings and karabiners, 30m rope.
FIRST ASCENT: unknown.

At the beginning of the seventeenth century, a well-known German astronomer called Baron de Zach caused great amusement among the scientific community when he claimed to have seen the Canigou from Marseille, 253 kilometres away. The general incredulity with which this story was received lasted almost three-quarters of a century, until the truth behind the baron's strange observation was revealed. In fact, for one or two days every year, around 10 February and 28 October, an observer looking west from the basilica of Notre-Dame de la Garde will see the silhouette of the Canigou projected on to the golden orb of the sun as it sets below the horizon.

Of all the Pyrenees' major summits, the Canigou is undoubtedly the most 'maritime'. Situated a mere stone's throw from the Mediterranean and rising head and shoulders above the surrounding hills, it appears a little haughty, as if it has turned its back on the rest of the chain in order to flaunt its charms seawards to the wondering gaze of sailors and the gods of the deep. Long ago, many people believed it was the highest mountain in Europe. King Peter III of Catalonia-Aragon, who seems to have been a bit of a braggart, claimed to have made the first ascent of the Canigou in 1285. King Peter's adventure was recorded for posterity by an Italian monk called Fra Salimbene in an epic tale that is more akin to the myths that have surrounded the area's lakes and ridges since the dawn of time than a historical record. In these legends, found all across the Pyrenees, the mountains are wreaked by terrible storms and inhabited by terrifying monsters, ferocious dragons and diabolical forces that may be awoken simply by tossing a pebble into a lake.

Today, the Canigou has become an emblem of Catalonian unity that attracts thousands of hikers every summer, although they tend to be drawn more by the breathtaking views than by the idea of visiting an important symbol. This popularity is not without its disadvantages, but there is an alternative to the normal route for mountaineers looking for a quieter day out. The Quazemi Ridge rarely receives many visitors, allowing you to enjoy a more contemplative ascent before joining the exuberant and colourful masses at the summit. What is more, the easy-angled nature of the Quazemi Ridge means there are plenty of opportunities for soaking up the superb surroundings. Although the rock requires care where the climbing

Near the start, looking across to the summit of the Canigou.

CANIGOU MASSIF

The ridge seen from the Porteille de Valmanya.

The III+ descent.

is easy, it is good on the more difficult sections of the ridge, which are often short descents. As a result, a few slings and a short rope will provide all the reassurance you need to ensure this mini ridge remains a fun outing. And, as on Chamonix's Aiguille du Midi, where climbers topping-out from the Cosmiques Ridge are greeted by admiring glances from the tourists on the viewing platform, your arrival on this beautiful Catalonian summit will not go unnoticed.

QUAZEMI RIDGE

From the Marialles hut, go up the GR10 to around 2,000m, then follow the Canigou normal route (yellow waymarkers) until a short distance past the Arago hut. Turn off the path at around 2,200m and head north up the large, grassy slope to a subsidiary summit (2,721m) between Pic Quazemi and the Canigou. The ridge starts here. After a horizontal section, go down through a letterbox, then move back on to the crest. Avoid a difficult section by descending the south side of the ridge to a notch (III+) at the foot of a small gendarme. Climb the gendarme (III), then continue along the crest. Climb a final step (II+), then follow the ridge easily to the summit.

DESCENT

Climb down a chimney on the south-east side of the summit. Continue down a south-facing gully to the path that goes below the Porteille de Valmanya. Follow this path back to the hut (2½ hrs).

PEDRAFORCA (2,497m)

TRAVERSE OF THE THREE PEAKS
START POINT: Lluis Estasen Hut.
DIFFICULTY: PD. A few moves of grade-II climbing and an abseil from the lower peak. Two sections equipped with chains but still involving grade-III climbing.
TIMES: 6–7 hrs hut to hut.
VERTICAL HEIGHT: 1,150m for the round trip.
CONDITIONS: from late May until the first snow falls.
GEAR: 50m rope, a few slings and karabiners, abseil gear.
FIRST ASCENT: unknown.

The Pedraforca can seem like a mountain at the end of the world to French mountaineers. Not that the climate, vegetation or people are so different; it is more that these proud needles are tucked away in a hidden corner of the Spanish Pyrenees that is not easily reached from France. Catalan climbers, on the other hand, view this striking mountain with the admiration it deserves, promising themselves that one day they too will climb it.

Local people have long regarded the Pedraforca's striking crown with almost hallowed reverence, so it is somewhat surprising that the first ascensionists of the normal routes left no record of their exploits. As a result, the mountain did not make its first appearance in the annals of mountaineering until the epic conquest of the difficult north face in the 1920s and 1930s.

Despite the summit's modest altitude, there is also something slightly epic about the traverse of the three peaks, a truly grandiose expedition along which the scenery changes almost constantly as you move from face to face. The technical difficulties are modest and short-lived, but you will need to master a full range of rope techniques and be able to climb carrying coils if you are accompanying a less-experienced partner.

As an astute mountaineer you will know not to underestimate the length of the climb and to take care to look for the best line through the sometimes-complex terrain. However, the most important quality you will need is, perhaps, the ability to remain attentive for long periods of time, as the rock is sometimes unstable and requires almost constant care. On the other hand, the route is not particularly committing and it is possible to retreat at almost any moment by descending to

The Estasen hut and the flanks of the Pedraforca.

CATALONIA

The Pollego Inferior and El Calderer separated by the Enforcadura. The Pollego Superior is hidden behind El Calderer.

The 'La Dola' slab (II).

the Enforcadura (fork) between the two Pollegos (peaks) and then heading east down the long scree slope of the Tartera.

The elegant spires of the Pedraforca have not only inspired climbers. Pablo Picasso was so enchanted by the area that he spent a year in Gósol, the tiny village at the foot of the mountain. Another reason to pay homage to these noble peaks?

TRAVERSE

Head south-south-east from the hut along a path signposted to *Pedraforca por la tartera*. Go up from the foot of the large scree slope towards a huge boulder (1,800m) at the start of the path to the Pollego Inferior. Follow the green waymarkers steeply upwards (south-west) to the start of the ridge (2,020m) that leads to the lower peak. Go easily up the ridge, then climb the 'La Dola' slab (II) to get to the foot of the final step. Climb a gully with a chain. From the summit (2,400m), head west along the ridge to two abseil rings on its left (south) side, where it plunges steeply downwards. Do one 45m abseil or two 25m abseils to get to a gully. Go down this gully for a few metres, then gain a notch on the crest of the ridge. Move on to the north face and go down a steep gully to the large scree slope. This is the Enforcadura. Go up to the ridge linking the higher peak to El Calderer. Two steep steps below El Calderer are equipped with chains: the first step is about 30m high; the second step is smooth and narrow, so it is best to leave your rucksack at the bottom. From the summit (2,490m), retrace your steps to get to the Pollego Superior (2,497m). Follow the yellow waymarkers, first along the ridge crest and then down a steep gully with polished holds on the south side of the ridge (II). Go back up towards the ridge as far as the first crest.

Keep following the waymarkers to the third crest, avoiding any difficult sections via the south face, then go down steep gullies on the right (north) to the Coll del Verdet (II). Follow the yellow and white waymarkers back to the hut.

MONT VALIER (2,838m)

FAUSTIN COULOIR
START POINT: Aula bivouac hut (1,550m).
DIFFICULTY: AD+.
TIMES: 4–5 hrs for the climb.
VERTICAL HEIGHT: approx. 1,000m from the start of the Peyre Blanc valley to the Col de Faustin.
CONDITIONS: spring when the snowpack is stable.
GEAR: a few ice screws and pegs, slings, karabiners, possibly skis or snowshoes for the descent.
FIRST ASCENT: unknown.

Even though the Couserans massif lies within the official boundaries of the *département*, locals will always tell you 'they are not really part of the Ariège'. Perhaps it is the slightly different climate or a forgotten episode in history that gives people from this corner of the Pyrenees such pride in their identity. Towering high above this little fiefdom, Mont Valier is the undisputed 'Lord of the Couserans'. Its truncated peak lies slightly to the north of the main chain, making it both a superb viewpoint and an easily recognisable landmark, visible from all the major summits of the central Pyrenees. Supposedly climbed for the first time in the fifth century by Valerius, the bishop of Couserans, it is a popular summit in summer. However, once winter falls, few people venture into these wild mountains, deterred by the long, difficult and sometimes dangerous approach, and the absence of staffed huts. As a result, despite being so close to hand, the steep, snow-smoothed slopes of these untamed summits feel wonderfully remote, like distant lands, rarely trodden by humankind.

The Valier massif at dawn. The Col de Peyre Blanc and Petit Valier are on the right.

ARIÉGE PYRENEES

3

The Col de Peyre Blanc, Petit Valier and Mont Valier.

MONT VALIER
FAUSTIN COULOIR

The Faustin Couloir, on the east face of Mont Valier, is the most famous snow climb in the Ariège. In fact, ski mountaineers sometimes climb the Faustin as a way of accessing the superb ski descent down the neighbouring Peyre Blanc Couloir. Despite its modest altitude, it must not be taken lightly and a very early start is essential in order to minimise the risk from falling rocks, which regularly sweep down the initial gully as soon as the sun hits the upper slopes. In addition, the slopes are highly avalanche prone, so the Faustin should only be attempted when the snow pack is stable. But, choose the right day and you are sure to look back on your ascent of this legendary mountain as one of the highlights of your mountaineering career.

FAUSTIN COULOIR
From the hut, go back down the GR10 for about 200m, then turn left and contour above the forest to gain the middle of the Peyre Blanc valley at about 1,570m. It is a good idea to reconnoitre this approach the day before. Head west/north-west up the slope to the foot of the couloir, which starts at about 2,100m (sections at up to 40°). If there is not much snow, there may be an open bergschrund below the couloir. Climb a section exposed to stone fall (45/50°) to get to a jammed block. Getting round the block is not too difficult (70/80°) if there is a lot of snow, but this section can involve some delicate mixed climbing if the snow cover is thin. It is also possible to climb the rock on the right (IV+) and then go up a ramp to a sling belay. A final, easier-angled wall (50/55°) leads to the gentler slopes (40°) below the Col de Faustin. Continue easily from the col to the summit (30 mins).

DESCENT
Go back down to the Col de Faustin and climb the Petit Valier. Go down to the Col de Peyre Blanc, then descend the couloir (40°) on the east side of the col. Keep heading east to get to the Pas de Clauère (1,868m) and the Aula hut.

The last few metres of the couloir.

ARIÉGE PYRENEES 3

Starting the final slope.

PICO DE ANETO (3,404m)

SALENQUES-TEMPESTADES RIDGE
START POINT: bivouac beside Ibón de Barrancs at the top of the Ésera Valley.
DIFFICULTY: D/D+. Long and committing climb, retreat difficult, requires experience in moving quickly along ridges.
TIMES: 7–8 hrs of climbing from the Collado de Salenques.
VERTICAL HEIGHT: 750m for the ridge.
CONDITIONS: the long descent from the summit is much easier at the beginning of the season when the ground is still covered in snow.
GEAR: 50m rope, slings, set of nuts, a few cams, crampons, ice axe.
FIRST ASCENT: first full traverse: R. Ollivier and H. Wild, 1934. Tempestades Ridge: Count of Ussel with the guides Castagné and Haurillón, 1912. Salenques Ridge: J. Arlaud and C. Laffont, 1922.

On 20 July 1842, just as they were congratulating themselves on a well-deserved triumph, the first ascensionists of the Aneto found their way to the summit blocked by a final and unexpected obstacle. Albert de Franqueville named this exposed, 30-metre arête of rock 'Muhammad's Bridge'. Why this seemingly enigmatic name? The answer can be found in the Koran, as the bridge in question is the As-Sirat, which stretches over Hell and leads directly to Heaven but which is 'thinner than a hair and sharper than a sabre'. In the words of the prophet: 'Some will cross in the blink of an eye. Some will cross like the wind or a bolt of lightning. Some will cross like the birds. Others will cross on their knees, or on their bellies. Others will fall and hang on with their hands and cross in this way.' Applied to the final ridge of the Aneto, the prophecy may seem a little overstated, although the analogy appears more apt on busy summer days, when queues of people are scrambling over this section.

The ridge at dawn viewed from the Collado de Salenques.

MONTES MALDITOS

Crossing Muhammad's Bridge may provide a modest test for novice mountaineers, but it does not involve any real technical climbing. In fact, the Koranic parable would be better suited to the Salenques-Tempestades Ridge, on the other side of the mountain, where a series of steep pinnacles, imposing walls and complex terrain seem to have been created with the sole intention of frustrating the efforts of climbers trying to reach this marvellous and much-sought-after summit. Only a few routes in the Pyrenees are long enough and remote enough to require a bivouac, and this is one of the best – a long, high-altitude scramble that culminates at the summit of the highest peak in the chain.

Most climbers choose to bivouac at the lake (Ibón de Barrancs, 2,380 metres) near the top of the Ésera Valley, from where the summit can be reached in a day, allowing you to leave your bivouac gear near the lake and pick it up on the descent. However, it would be a shame not to take the opportunity to spend a night at altitude by bivouacking on the summit of Pico de Margalide, perfectly situated in the middle of the traverse. Sleeping on this magnificent promontory at an altitude of 3,244 metres provides an unparalleled – and quite rare – feeling of isolation.

The summit Virgin shrouded in ice.

PICO DE ANETO
SALENQUES-TEMPESTADES RIDGE

The only drawback, because there is always a drawback, is the need to carry heavy sacks containing all your bivouac gear and water. This means you will climb more slowly, but this inconvenience is more than offset by the advantage of having more time to savour the solitude and appreciate the wonderful atmosphere of this long journey through these grandiose mountains. Another advantage of sleeping on the ridge is that it means you don't have to make a pre-dawn start from Ibón de Barrancs and then navigate in the dark across the complex and confusing terrain that leads to the ridge.

The most difficult climbing is concentrated in the first part of the route. A few sections of unstable rock after Pico de Margalide can be avoided by staying on the south side of the crest, but there is no way to avoid the loose and exposed ledges on the descent via the Brecha de Tempestades. Once at the end of the traverse, it is possible to prolong the feeling of solitude by descending via Plan d'Aiguallut or, better still, via Ibón del Salterillo, rather than following the normal route.

APPROACH
From the lake, head south up the left bank of the valley towards a large moraine that runs straight up to the Collado de Salenques. Follow the crest of the moraine to a flatter section below an area of rock. Avoid the rock by heading diagonally leftwards up a steep section, then bear rightwards slightly to regain the crest of the moraine just west of the pass.

SALENQUES-TEMPESTADES RIDGE
The first part of the climb, along the west side of the ridge, is easy (II). Go up a gully to a notch. Cross on to the east face, then follow the ridge crest to the foot of a gendarme. Climb diagonally rightwards across the gendarme (III+) for about 25m, then traverse right before its summit to get to a saddle (40m, IV). Go in front of, or through, a hole in the ridge to reach the foot of the second gendarme. Climb it directly (IV), then continue up less steep ground on the right. Climb a chimney on the west face (III) to get to the top of the next step. Abseil (10m) into a notch on the other side of the gendarme. Continue easily to the foot of another step. Climb a 25m pitch (IV-) to get to a steep wall (25m, IV) below the top of a gendarme. Follow the ridge more easily (II/III), then go along ledges on the east face to the summit of Pico de Margalide, where the ridge curves west.

Easy climbing (II) on the left-hand side of the ridge leads to Pico de Tempestades. Continue along the ridge, going round the south side of a gendarme (II) and then heading right round a short step. Move back on to the crest of the ridge at the gendarmes before the Brecha de Tempestades (III+). Follow ledges of very loose rock, then go down to a notch. Move on to the other face. Turn a steep wall on the left (III), then traverse left along a horizontal crack. Go over blocks to get to the flank of a spur, which is followed to the main ridge (III+). Climb a final step to get on to the shoulder, then continue up increasingly easy ground to the summit of the Aneto.

MONTES MALDITOS 4

Looking back along the ridge from the summit of the Aneto.

'Muhammad's Bridge' and the summit after an August snowstorm.

PICO DE LA MALADETA (3,308m)

NORTH–SOUTH TRAVERSE
START POINT: Rencluse Hut.
DIFFICULTY: PD+. Snow climb, then a traverse on sometimes-poor rock.
TIMES: 4 hrs to the summit, 1½ hrs for the traverse to the Collado Maldito.
VERTICAL HEIGHT: 1,170m from the hut.
CONDITIONS: as long as there is still snow in the couloir below the Collado de la Rimaya (usually until early July).
GEAR: crampons, ice axe, 50m rope, five slings, a few nuts, five karabiners and four quickdraws.
FIRST ASCENTS: via the Glaciar de la Maladeta: F. Parrot and P. Barrau, 29 September 1817. Traverse to the Collado Maldito: unknown.

As dawn broke on 11 August 1824, a group of three men left the hut near the Plan d'Están where they had passed the night. They were on their way to the Maladeta. The two young engineers were full of confidence because their guide, Pierre Barrau, knew these mountains like the back of his hand. Now sixty-eight years old, Barrau had an outstanding reputation. Had he not done the first ascent of this mountain seven years earlier?

The climb went smoothly until the three men got to the glacier, where they found a gaping bergschrund blocking their route into the final gully. Barrau hadn't brought a rope. Overconfidence or just an oversight? No matter. They tested the snow bridges with the points of their alpenstocks, chose one that seemed to be sturdy enough, and Barrau started to cross. Suddenly, the snow collapsed under his weight. 'My God! I'm lost! I'm drowning!' were, it seems, the last words he cried as he fell into the chasm. It took 107 years for the glacier to relinquish his body, which finally emerged from the glacier tongue, 1,100 metres lower down the valley.

This terrible accident came as a great shock to the mountaineers of the day, who were so profoundly affected that most became extremely wary of venturing on to the area's glaciers, and the race to conquer the great summits of the Pyrenees lay dormant for more than fifteen years. As a result, it was not until 1842, fifty-six years after the first ascent of Mont Blanc, that Pico de Aneto was finally conquered. Even then, the first ascensionists tackled the mountain via its south face, carefully avoiding the ice on the opposite side.

The 'Barrau bergschrund'.

Today, the north-facing couloir between the bergschrund and the Collado de la Rimaya is rarely in condition after the first few days of July, so it is more popular with ski mountaineers in spring than with climbers in summer. Nevertheless, the seriousness of the route should not be underestimated. The rock ridge above the Collado Maldito, approached from the south, provides the normal route for most of the summer season. The traverse described here combines these two routes to give a wonderfully varied outing. It also provides very fit climbers with the option of continuing from the Collado Maldito to the top of the Aneto, rather than descending straight back to the valley, and thereby completing a magnificent but extremely long circuit over two of the highest peaks in the Pyrenees.

MONTES MALDITOS

Above: Looking across to the Maladeta massif from the Port de Vénasque.

Below: The upper section of the couloir.

NORTH–SOUTH TRAVERSE

From the Rencluse hut, head due south to the Glaciar de la Maladeta. Go up the glacier to the foot of a large, snowy couloir that comes down from the ridge just to the right of the summit. Be careful crossing the bergschrund, which is sometimes hidden under a treacherously thin layer of snow. Climb the couloir, then follow the easy ridge to the summit. The route should only be attempted when the couloir is full of snow, as the rock is extremely loose and unstable. From the summit, head south across an easy scree slope, then follow the cairns down the jagged ridge, staying mostly on its western side. Much of the descent to the Collado Maldito is over jumbled boulders, some of which are loose (sections of grade II and III climbing). Once at the pass, head north across the glacier to the Portillón Superior (2,890m). Go over the saddle and follow the ascent route back to the hut.

PIC DE MAUPAS (3,109m)

WEST RIDGE

START POINT: Maupas Hut.
DIFFICULTY: AD-.
TIMES: 3½–4 hrs; descent to the hut 2 hrs.
VERTICAL HEIGHT: 750m
CONDITIONS: early in the season while the slope is still covered in snow. The route should be avoided when ice starts to appear.
GEAR: crampons with anti-balling plates, ice axe, rope, slings, a few nuts, karabiners and quickdraws.
FIRST ASCENT: H. and A. Barrué, and Leclère-Chavad, 1929.

Places are just like people: some you take an instant dislike to, others you immediately fall in love with. For me, a tiny corner of the mountains, hidden in the far reaches of the Cirque des Crabioules, falls into the latter category, and I can't really explain why. Perhaps it is because it is too far from any normal route to receive many visitors. Or it could be because the valiant remnants of the area's glaciers magnify the severity of the steep cliffs that rise above them. And it may be because the cirque has such a bleak atmosphere and feels so isolated from the rest of the world.

In addition to these intangible charms, the austere but strangely welcoming west face of Pic de Maupas is home to the best (and one of the only) mixed route in the Luchon area. The route is easy to find due to the distinctive shape of the snowy crest that has to be climbed to get to the frontier ridge. Viewed from a distance and from straight on, the line looks very intimidating, but you shouldn't let appearances undermine your confidence, as there are few technical difficulties to overcome if snow conditions are good. All you have to do is move together correctly, which means staying close together, taking care when placing your feet, making sure snow does not ball-up under your crampons, and using your ice axe properly. In fact, it is an excellent route on which to practise these basic techniques in preparation for longer and more challenging climbs.

What is more, the angle of the snow on the initial slopes increases slowly, so less confident climbers have time to get used to the terrain and to start feeling at home before they reach the steepest slopes. The hardest part of the route is moving on to the rock ridge from the top of the snow slope. Protection is difficult to place on this section, although a few old pegs can still be found, and the difficulties are short lived if there is a lot of snow. The ridge itself is quite straightforward, apart from an exposed section that can give beginners food for thought, as it has to be climbed by straddling the very narrow and exposed ridge crest.

The steep section between the glacier and the ridge.

LUCHON AREA

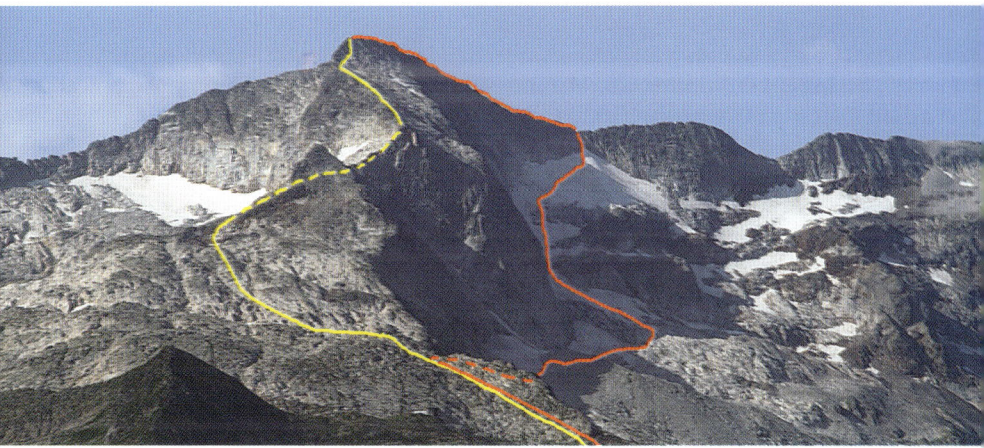

Pic de Maupas seen from Superbagnères.

Parts of the ridge are quite airy.

At the start of the glacier.

WEST RIDGE

From the hut, follow the base of the ridge southwards to around 2,575m. Go down an exposed path for about 60m into the Cirque des Crabioules, then traverse south-west below the north face of the Maupas (beware of stone fall). Go up the small glacier at the foot of the west face to a snowy spur that starts at around 2,800m. Climb this spur (100m at up to 35°) to the frontier ridge. Depending on snow cover, the final section of the slope below the ridge may be bare rock (up to 50m, III+ max, difficult to place protection but there are a few *in situ* pegs). Follow the frontier ridge (III max, narrow in places) to the summit of Pic de Maupas (3½–4 hrs from the hut).

DESCENT

Several rocky gullies can be descended (II) to get to the north slope (normal route). Follow the ridge on the right-hand side of this slope to a small notch. Go down the rock on the right. Gain the saddle between Pic de Maupas and Tusse de Maupas (II+) by descending the 'bad step' ('mauvais pas' in French, 'mau-pas' in local patois) that gave the peak its name. Snow (30° slope) can persist until the middle of the season, making this section more difficult. Go down either the crest of the ridge or the eastern slopes of the Tusse to the hut.

CIRQUE DU PORTILLON

People who would like to see what an archetypal glacial valley looks like could choose no better place to go than the Oô Valley. Here they will find every glacial landform imaginable – glacial lakes, glacial sills, moraines, folds, erratics – laid out as in a textbook illustration. Of the ancient glaciers that slowly sculpted and chiselled these mountains over the centuries, all that remain today are a few remnants, bravely hanging on below the ridges of the Cirque du Portillon. It is difficult to imagine that these sheets of ice were once big enough to power the formidable erosion machine that shaped this basin, and how much longer these vestiges of another age will survive, no one knows. Due to climate change, they are diminishing under our very eyes, leaving larger and larger areas of rock exposed at the end of every summer. In fact, the glaciers have retreated completely from the faces with more easterly and westerly aspects, uncovering some excellent climbs.

The Cirque du Portillon lies at the very top of this great glacial basin, enclosed by a wall of almost a dozen 3,000-metre peaks. One of the best vantage points from which to admire this ring of prestigious summits is the Tusse de Montarqué, which rises like a rostrum above two lakes of deepest blue in the middle of the cirque.

Few weaknesses break the formidable barrier of cliffs encircling the southern edge of the cirque and separating France from Spain. Mountain lovers of all types pass through the cirque every summer, many of whom make use of the mountain hut built at the end of the last century. Perched at an altitude of 2,500 metres, the hut caters to everyone, from tourists on day trips to hikers attempting the Pyrenees High-Level Route and rock climbers who have come up for several days to pit themselves against the area's best routes. In fact, there are not many places in the Pyrenees that offer such a variety of routes of all levels of difficulty, so the cirque's faces and ridges are an excellent training ground in which to try out climbs of different styles and to perfect one's techniques. The choice is wide and there are enough routes to occupy even the most avid climber for several visits.

Looking down the corner from B6 of the Grand Dièdre on Pic des Spijeoles.

Strong winds whip across the Crabioules-Lézat Ridge.

PIC DES CRABIOULES (3,116M)
PIC LÉZAT (3,107M)

CRABIOULES-LÉZAT RIDGE
START POINT: Portillon Hut.
DIFFICULTY: AD+. Good rock, very exposed climbing, retreat difficult.
TIMES: approach 1½ hrs; climb to the top of Pic Lézat 3½ hrs.
VERTICAL HEIGHT: 430m
CONDITIONS: from spring to autumn.
GEAR: 40m rope, set of nuts, set of cams, slings, karabiners.
FIRST ASCENT: J. Arlaud and C. Laffont, 1921.

First-time visitors to Superbagnères, the ski resort above Luchon, find themselves wide-eyed before the spectacular vista that opens up before them. A large part of the Pyrenean chain is visible from the plateau, although it is the imposing wall of rock between Pic de Sacroux and Pic du Quayrat that irresistibly draws the eye. As well as forming a natural barrier between France and Spain, this 10-kilometre precipice provides 'the most beautiful panorama in the Pyrenees', according to a local song, at least. Linking five summits above 3,000 metres and rarely descending below 2,500 metres, only the highest peaks of Spain's Montes Malditos emerge above the ridge, while a few remnant glaciers still find refuge at its foot.

At the start of the ridge.

Looking across from the summit to Pic de Maupas and Pic des Crabioules.

CIRQUE DU PORTILLON

Quayrat, Lézat, Crabioules and Royo surrounding Lac du Portillon.

PIC DES CRABIOULES, PIC LÉZAT
CRABIOULES-LÉZAT RIDGE

Although this long skyline ridge can be traversed in its entirety, most mountaineers are happy to divide it into shorter segments. The section from Pic de Boum to Pic de Maupas is a lovely climb, but pride of place goes to the traverse from Pic des Crabioules to Pic Lézat, where the elegance of the wall and the spectacular setting more than make up for the variable quality of the rock. The route can be started from the Maupas hut, but this option should only be attempted by fit and experienced mountaineers, as it is necessary to first climb the twin peaks of the Crabioules. Consequently, most climbers prefer to start from the Portillon hut, thereby minimising the length of both the approach and the descent.

Experience and a cool head are key success factors on ridge climbs, and this is particularly the case on the Crabioules-Lézat Ridge. Here, the exceptionally exposed terrain means you need to be much more than a good rock climber to tackle the traverse with confidence; you have to be able to move together safely, find protection on traverses and descents, choose the most solid holds when the rock is poor, and climb boldly when confronted with steep and exposed walls.

This long and strenuous outing is also a good test of fitness, so you should only attempt the route if you are sure you have the stamina needed to get the most from one of the best climbs in the area.

CRABIOULES-LÉZAT RIDGE
From the Portillon hut, go up the Litérole Valley to the top of the big moraine (45 mins). Climb the broken rocks on the left to get to the notch to the left of the western summit of Pic des Crabioules (Brèche Mamy). Continue along the ridge to its lowest point, going over a series of needles but avoiding some of the descents by moving on to the Lis side of the crest (II+).

Avoid the first gendarme by following a narrow and exposed ledge on the south face. Belay at the foot of the Gendarme Blanc. Traverse round the Litérole side of this gendarme, going over a distinctive block that protrudes from the south corner (III+).

Climb a 40m wall (II+), then continue across boulders. Climb another wall (15m, III) to get to the foot of a steep step, which is climbed via the wide crack on its left-hand side (III+). Belay at the foot of a large, square block. Descend the gully on the right for about 10m, then go up to the foot of a slab, which is climbed by a crack on the right (II+). Continue over boulders to the final wall (short but steep, III+). Continue to the top of the gully of the normal route, which is followed easily to the summit.

DESCENT
Go back down the ridge for about 200m to a cairn at the top of a steep gully. Go straight down at first, then do several leftwards (east) traverses to get to the top of a large scree slope. Traverse right, descending slightly to get to the top of another gully. Go down this gully and the grassy slopes below to join the approach route approximately 15 minutes from the hut (1½ hrs from the summit to the hut).

Left: A narrow and very exposed ridge.
Right: On the traverse below the Gendarme Blanc.

CIRQUE DU PORTILLON

PIC DES SPIJEOLES (3,065m)

SOUTH-EAST RIDGE
START POINT: Espingo Hut.
DIFFICULTY: AD+.
TIMES: approach 2 hrs; climb 4 hrs.
VERTICAL HEIGHT: 400m
CONDITIONS: from spring to autumn.
GEAR: slings, set of nuts and set of cams, five quickdraws, seven karabiners.
FIRST ASCENT: M. Jeannel and Pouech, 1937.

In the 1960s, the only times my father went into the mountains were to fish for trout or hunt Pyrenean chamois. Then, one morning he was sitting in the kitchen of the Espingo hut when a mountain-guide friend, who had been left in the lurch by a client, offered to take him up the south-east ridge of the Spijeoles. My father immediately accepted, even though he had no idea of what he was letting himself in for. It seems he did quite well. He was certainly pleased enough with himself to tell me and my brothers the story in great detail, over and over again. So, even before I ever set foot on the route, I knew by heart every nook and cranny of the Aiguille Jeannel, the layback on the vertical wall, and the tiny holds on the black slab.

Despite never doing another climb in his life, my father immediately began referring to the guide in question as 'my favourite guide'. Whatever the guide's other qualities, he had good taste when it came to picking routes, as the climbing on the south-east ridge of the Spijeoles is excellent and its reputation is thoroughly deserved. It is, perhaps, the very structure of the mountain that makes this route so good. The first part, to the top of the Aiguille Jeannel, follows slabs and cracks on a steep, wide wall and does not feel at all like a ridge climb. This contrasts nicely with the section above, which is more of a classic ridge: easier angled, narrow, elegant and exposed.

CIRQUE DU PORTILLON

Left: On the Aiguille Jeannel, high above Lac Saussat and the Espingo hut.
Right: The east wall of the Spijeoles.

PIC DES SPIJEOLES
SOUTH-EAST RIDGE

Climbers on the second pitch.

In addition, its position, towering above Lac Glacé, one of the most beautiful lakes in the valley, undoubtedly adds to the route's charm, with the lake waters appearing to lap against the foot of the ridge and the huge and impressively vertical east face. Finally, the climbing is exceptionally varied, with delicate slabs and strenuous walls alternating to produce a superb route that is a must for every Pyrenean mountaineer.

SOUTH-EAST RIDGE
From the hut, head south along the Lac du Portillon path to the footbridge at the Coume de l'Abesque, at 2,100m. Turn right (west) at the bridge to follow the Pic des Spijeoles normal route. The south-east ridge is to the left of the summit. Go up easy ground to gain the foot of the ridge (at about 2,700m). Traverse right along a grassy ledge to a corner, which is climbed to a belay on a large ledge of red schist (40m, IV, two peg runners, B1, two pegs). Climb the schist, trending slightly rightwards to gain the crest of the ridge and a large ledge (25m, III, B2). Go up the ridge. Trend slightly leftwards at first (one move IV, one peg), then head back right to a large ledge (35m, IV, then II, B3). Two easy pitches lead to the summit of the Aiguille Jeannel (40m, then 45m, II to III, B5). Descend to a notch, then go over a needle and climb another pitch (40m, II). Climb a scree-filled gully to the foot of a steep wall (B6, two pegs), which is climbed directly (10m, IV+, one peg, B7). Go up slightly rightwards to a large ledge at the foot of a black slab (30m, II, B8). Climb the slab via a rightwards-leaning crack (20m, IV-, B9).

The serrated upper section of the ridge is less steep and can be followed without difficulty. The climb finishes at the large scree slope below the summit, which can be gained by following the normal route or by continuing up the ridge.

The second part of the ridge is more exposed.

CIRQUE DU PORTILLON

Looking across the black slab to Lac Glacé and Pic du Seil de la Baque.

PIC DES SPIJEOLES (3,065m)

GRAND DIÈDRE
START POINT: Espingo Hut.
DIFFICULTY: D. Mostly crack and corner climbing, one grade-V slab move and an awkward, IV+ crack. A steep snowfield usually persists below the foot of the route until the middle of the season, so crampons may be needed for the approach.
TIMES: approach 2 hrs; climb 3½ hrs.
VERTICAL HEIGHT: 300m for the climb.
CONDITIONS: from June to October, as soon as the face is dry. Beware of stone fall if there are other teams on the route.
GEAR: crampons (early in the season), one ice axe for the party, rock shoes, two 50m ropes, slings, four karabiners, eight quickdraws, helmet, nuts and cams to back up the numerous *in situ* pegs.
FIRST ASCENT: F. Céréza and L. Malus, September 1946.

The start of P3.

A huge granite wall, 250–300 metres high, dominates the western side of the vast Cirque d'Espingo. This is the east face of Pic des Spijeoles, a superb, sunny cliff that has attracted climbers since the early 1940s. There are now a dozen routes on the face, the most recent of which was first climbed in 2006. The Grand Dièdre follows the huge groove that slices through the right-hand side of the cliff, unfailingly drawing the eye. It is easy to work out the line of the route, just follow the crack from the foot of the face to the huge, open-book corner that splits the upper part of the wall. As the most logical and most aesthetic line on the cliff, it has, quite understandably, become the most classic and most popular route in the area. The climbing is reassuring, enclosed but never confined and on excellent, rough rock. In addition, route finding is straightforward and natural protection is easy to place whenever it is needed to complement the abundant *in situ* gear, so you can relax and concentrate on enjoying the moves. As for the crux – every route has to have a crux – it is where it should be, near the top, where a smooth and exposed slab will test your footwork. That being said, for me, the hardest part of the climb is the awkward chimney on pitch five.

CIRQUE DU PORTILLON

PIC DES SPIJEOLES
GRAND DIÈDRE

A steep snowfield can block access to the foot of the face until quite late in the season, so it is worth asking the hut warden whether or not you are likely to need an ice axe and crampons to get to the route. The only black spot comes from the climb's popularity. If there are other teams on the route, which is often the case, climbers below them can be exposed to stone fall. Given the nature of the terrain, any stones climbers dislodge tend to channel down the route, which is a very good reason for starting the two-hour walk-in very early and making sure you are at the head of the queue.

GRAND DIÈDRE

From the hut, head south along the Lac du Portillon path to the footbridge at the Coume de l'Abesque, at 2,100m. Turn right (west) and go up to the east face of the Spijeoles. In some years, the snowfield at the foot of the wall does not melt until the middle of August. Go up the snowfield and a band of schist (III) to get to the start of the route. Climb a wall of red and white rock to get to the large corner.

Below the grade-V move on P10.

CIRQUE DU PORTILLON

P1: 45m, III.
P2: 25m, III+.
P3: 40m, IV. Continue for another 15m, then move out of the corner to climb a steep, dark wall on the right. Move back into the corner above this wall.
P4: 30m, III.
P5: 20m, IV+.
P6: 30m, III. Belay on the left on a good ledge.
P7: 50m, IV, then II+.
P8: 55m, II+, then IV.
P9: 35m, IV.
P10: 35m, V. Follow the corner, then traverse right into the middle of the slab.
P11: 45m, IV. Climb the black crack above the belay.

Nearing the belay at the top of P2.

PIC DES GOURGS BLANCS (3,129m)

VIA PIC JEAN ARLAUD
START POINT: Portillon Hut.
DIFFICULTY: PD+ for the rock section. Climbers must be able to place natural protection and master basic mountaineering techniques. The rock at the top of the descent gully is very loose and difficult to protect. The difficulty of the glacier varies greatly depending on snow cover. Two 50m ropes are needed for the descent via Pic Jean Arlaud.
TIMES: 5 hrs from the hut to the summit, variable for the descent.
VERTICAL HEIGHT: approx. 250m from the Port d'Oô.
CONDITIONS: before the Glacier des Gourgs Blancs is bare ice.
GEAR: two 50m ropes, crampons, ice axe, abseil gear for the descent, slings, karabiners.
FIRST ASCENT: Bazillac, de Monts, Russell and Célestin Passet, 1864.

The old Ollivier guidebook, the Pyrenean climber's bible, was already noting the unwelcome consequences of glacial retreat and underlining the increasing difficulty of the normal route on Pic des Gourgs Blancs at the beginning of the 1970s. Forty-five years later, the situation has not improved. In fact, Pic des Gourgs Blancs is one of the summits in the Pyrenees where mountaineering has been most severely impacted by the thinning of the ice over the last twenty years. News of numerous failures on the normal route quickly spread round the valleys, destroying the reputation of a once-classic climb that is now rarely attempted.

Fortunately for climbers, the summit can still be reached via the neighbouring Pic Jean Arlaud. This route is slightly longer and more difficult than the old normal route, but it is one of the most enjoyable climbs in the Cirque du Portillon. As such, it has become a much sought-after prize for novice climbers, who are attracted by the magnificent setting, varied climbing and the finish on a truly majestic summit. Nevertheless, their desire to climb the line is often mixed with a little trepidation, as, viewed from the Tusse de Montarqué, traversed during the approach in the enchanting light of dawn, the peak looks anything but welcoming. However, its demeanour gradually softens as you

Below the Col du Pluviomètre, looking across to Pic Jean Arlaud and Pic des Gourgs Blancs.

CIRQUE DU PORTILLON

The remnants of the Glacier des Gourgs Blancs.

cross the Col du Pluviomètre and head towards the Col des Gourgs Blancs. Then, after the stiff climb to the Port d'Oô, the seemingly impregnable east face of Pic Jean Arlaud finally loses its forbidding aura and the easy-angled nature of the rock becomes apparent. In fact, the climbing is quite easy and the most exacting part of the route is the descent, which is very exposed and on highly unstable terrain. Great care is needed here, but this does not take anything away from the pleasure of climbing such a superb peak.

ROUTE DESCRIPTION
Head west from the hut to the Tusse de Montarqué. Traverse south across the summit and descend the ridge that runs to Pic du Seil de la Baque. Follow this ridge to the Col du Pluviomètre, then cross into the bowl below the Col des Gourgs Blancs. Go up a steep scree slope to the Port d'Oô. From the pass, traverse right across grassy ledges to the foot of two gullies. Climb the second gully (II/III, 55m), then go up the scree slope above to some slabs. Climb these slabs to get to the summit ridge and then the summit of Pic Jean Arlaud. Go down the west ridge (II) of Pic Jean Arlaud, at first on its left-hand side (south). An abseil may be necessary to get to the saddle between Pic Jean Arlaud and Pic des Gourgs Blancs. Continue easily up towards the Gourgs Blancs.

DESCENT
If the glacier is covered in snow, the best descent is via the old normal route. Go back to the saddle and (very carefully) descend the north couloir for about 60m to an *in situ* abseil station. The rock is very unstable, so the party should short-rope this section, staying close together and keeping the rope tight. When everyone has got to the abseil station, do a 30m abseil to get to the bergschrund. Crampons are often needed to descend the first part of the glacier safely. Late in the season, when there is little snow left on the glacier, the descent is even more difficult and dangerous, and excellent crampon technique (or an abseil) will be needed. Retrace your footsteps from below the Col des Gourgs Blancs to the hut.

Glacier retreat means that this descent is now only practicable early in the season, so there are plans to set up an abseil line on the east face of Pic Jean Arlaud. Ask at the hut for details.

PICO DE POSETS (3,375m)

ESPADAS RIDGE
START POINT: Angel Orus Hut.
DIFFICULTY: PD, very exposed ridge.
TIMES: 5 hrs from the hut to the summit.
VERTICAL HEIGHT: 1,300m from the hut, including 400m for the ridge.
CONDITIONS: from spring to autumn.
GEAR: crampons and ice axe at the beginning of the season, 30m rope, slings, a few nuts and karabiners.
FIRST ASCENT: unknown.

Carved from thick layers of folded marls and limestones, the contours of the Posets massif appear unsoftened by time and, wandering over the rugged and desolate summits of the second highest massif in the Pyrenees, it is easy to imagine you are exploring the primeval Earth. Even the vegetation has been defeated by the harshness of the environment, so hardy souls prepared to confront this barren desert of jagged ridges find themselves in the midst of an almost lunar landscape. The massif gets its name from the word *poset* (sometimes written *pocet*), meaning hole or cavity, in reference to the innumerable caves and cracks that riddle the bedrock and into which rainfall disappears the moment it touches the ground.

Pico de Posets, the second highest peak in the Pyrenees, is surrounded by three mountain huts, which provide the starting points for the three normal routes. These routes vary in difficulty, but the most enjoyable way to reach the summit is via the ridge over the Pico Espadas. Most people start the route from the Cuello de Èristé, but the most interesting section starts a little higher, near Tucòn Royo. The climbing is technically straightforward, so the route should be within the capabilities of any experienced hiker. In fact, if it were not perched so high, it could even be considered easy. Moreover, the narrow and rocky itinerary over the lofty summit of the Espadas is unusually vertiginous, and the lack of handholds and the exposure on the razor-sharp ridge are likely to intimidate novice climbers.

Sunset on Pico Espadas.

POSETS MASSIF

The immense view towards Pico de Eristé and the Cotiella massif.

PICO DE POSETS
ESPADAS RIDGE

However, this is no reason to be put off, as there is little danger and with a modicum of encouragement you will soon start feeling confident enough to enjoy the magnificent views that spread out on all sides. And, after more than two hours immersed in this magical trail, you will emerge, liberated and euphoric, on to the summit of Pico de Posets.

ESPADAS RIDGE

From the hut, head north-west along the GR11 to the Llardaneta stream. Go past the stream and head north up the path to Pico de Posets. At around 2,650m, at the entrance to a defile called the Rue Royale, turn off the path and go up the grass and scree slope on the left. Bear north, then head west to go round the small summit at 2,891m. Continue heading west to Paso Tucòn Royo.

Just below the summit, looking back to Pico Espadas.

POSETS MASSIF

Follow the ridge northwards to Pico Espadas (one move of grade II). The route continues in a similar vein, but the ridge is more horizontal and more exposed. Climb a short wall (II+) on the traverse of Tuca de Llardaneta and Tuqueta Roya, then descend to the Corredor de J. Arlaud. From here, go up an easy scree slope to the summit of Pico de Posets.

DESCENT

Head due south along the ridge, then go south-west down a scree slope to the Cuello del Diente. Go down the gully to the south to a flatter area. Follow the Rue Royale to where it joins the approach route.

PIC DE NÉOUVIELLE (3,091m)

TROIS CONSEILLERS RIDGE
START POINT: Lac d'Aubert or Glère Hut.
DIFFICULTY: AD. At the beginning of the season, an ice axe and crampons may be needed for the snowfield below the Brèche de Néouvielle (Cap de Long side).
TIMES: approach 2–3 hrs; climb 2 hrs; descent 1½–2 hrs.
VERTICAL HEIGHT: approx. 160m for the ridge.
CONDITIONS: from spring to autumn.
GEAR: slings, a few nuts and cams, quickdraws, karabiners, ice axe and crampons until early summer.
FIRST ASCENT: H. Brulle, R. de Monts and C. Passet, 1891.

Pic de Néouvielle rises to a height of 3,091m and reigns over one of France's oldest nature reserves, created in 1936. Néouvielle means old snow, a reference to the snowfields that dot its slopes, and therefore the normal route, until late into the year. Nevertheless, the glaciers that used to flow down the mountain's northern flanks have long-since disappeared, so only the numerous lakes (there are more than seventy in the area) and stands of mountain pines, which grow at record altitudes here, break up the uniform colour of this granite landscape. The Trois Conseillers Ridge lies on the sunny side of the mountain, dividing the huge Lac de Cap de Long at the foot of the south face from the wonderful rock climbs on the west face.

This little climb is much more than a beginner's route; it is a veritable journey through the heights of the massif. With consistently excellent rock, easy-to-place protection and a relatively short section of technical climbing, it is possible to adopt a relaxed approach and enjoy the magnificent surroundings. These advantages combine to make it one of the most popular climbs in the Pyrenees, on which novice teams are regularly seen revelling in the climbing while testing their newly learnt skills. The foot of the ridge can be reached either from Barèges via the Glère hut, or from Lac d'Aubert, although a snowfield below the ledge leading to the notch can make this second option more difficult early in the season. The rock is always solid and enjoyable to climb, on both the steeper walls and the easier-angled sections, which are more exposed and have to be negotiated by straddling the very apex of the ridge. However, the icing on the cake is at the top, in the form of a highly featured slab you wish would go on forever. In fact, if you really are hungry for more when you get to the summit, you can always round off the day with an ascent of the Ferbos Ridge on the Pic des Trois Conseillers.

Pic Long, Monte Perdido and the summits of Gavarnie can be seen in the far distance.

NÉOUVIELLE MASSIF

Above: Pic des Trois Conseillers, Pic de Néouvielle and Pic Ramoun seen from the Cap de Long side.

Left: The lovely slab on pitch 7 (III+).

APPROACH FROM THE LAC D'AUBERT

From the Lac d'Aubert car park, go across the dam and follow the Néouvielle footpath to around 2,250m. Bear left (south) and follow the path (red and white waymarkers) to the Pas du Gat (2,465m). Descend towards Lac de Cap de Long for about 80m, then head west along the path below the Crête des Laquettes to a small cirque from where the ledge leading to the Brèche de Néouvielle can be seen clearly. Go up to the foot of the ledge. Cross the snowfield, or go round its right-hand side to get past the bergschrund, then go up the ledge to the notch (II, exposed). 2½–3 hrs.

APPROACH FROM THE GLÈRE HUT

From the Glère Hut, follow the path to the Brèche de Chausenque, then traverse below the west face of the Néouvielle to the Brèche de Néouvielle. 2 hrs.

TROIS CONSEILLERS RIDGE

P1: climb the steep crest of the ridge (50m, III).
P2: go left round a gendarme, then go through a notch to belay on a ledge on the south side (40m, III).
P3: climb a steep wall to get back on to the crest of the ridge, which is followed to the start of a more horizontal section (40m, III).
P4: continue along the ridge, staying mostly on the north side, to a corner (50m, III).
P5: climb the corner (IV), or go through the narrow 'letter box' on the right, then move back on to the crest (20m, III).
P6: continue more easily to an enormous, prow-shaped block. Belay at the foot of the prow, on the south side of the ridge (120m, II).
P7: climb the short wall and superb, highly featured slab above (30m, III+).
P8: follow the horizontal ridge to the summit (100m, II).

DESCENT

Follow the normal route to Lac d'Aubert (large snowfield to cross at the beginning of the season). If you started from the Glère Hut, turn off the normal route at around 2,750m and head north-west to go over the Brèche de Chausenque to the hut.

PIC DE LA MUNIA (3,133m)

TROUMOUSE RIDGE

START POINT: Cirque de Troumouse.
DIFFICULTY: PD+. Several sections of grade-II and grade-III climbing, some sections are exposed and difficult to protect.
TIMES: 10 hrs for the full circuit.
VERTICAL HEIGHT: 650m for the climb (total height gain: 1,150m).
CONDITIONS: generally early summer.
GEAR: rope, crampons, helmet, slings, a few nuts and quickdraws.
FIRST ASCENT: unknown.

Troumouse, Estaubé and Gavarnie – a unique trilogy of mountain cirques, a chain of three enormous horseshoes along the crest of the Pyrenees. If the dramatic immensity of Gavarnie's encircling wall excites awe in all who see it, the gentler relief of the Cirque d'Estaubé tends to evoke a more contemplative response. Troumouse, the easternmost cirque in the trilogy, combines features of both its neighbours, as if it had been custom made to satisfy visitors of every sensibility. The wide central valley is folded into a thousand nooks and crannies, many of which house tiny lakes surrounded by lush meadows on which cows and marmots lazily graze. But, continue up the valley and the gentle slopes abruptly give way to damp, grey crags that cast a dour eye over this little corner of paradise.

Pic de la Munia is the highest summit along this imposing barrier and a popular objective for Pyrenean mountaineers. A few snow slopes and the famous Pas du Chat add a little spice to the normal route, but more experienced mountaineers are likely to find the traverse of the ridge from the Col de la Sède a more satisfying adventure.

The ridge over Pic de Troumouse.

CIRQUE DE TROUMOUSE

The eastern half of the Cirque de Troumouse, from the Col de la Sède to the Col de la Munia.

Approaching the foot of the Serre Mourène.

The ridge is never difficult and has only a few sections of technical climbing; however, good mountaineering skills are needed to safely negotiate the sometimes loose and extremely exposed ground. In fact, the most important quality on this very long climb is an ability to remain focused and attentive, as the constantly steep drops on either side of the ridge will not forgive the slightest false step.

Peak-baggers looking to increase their tally of 3,000-metre summits will come away with an excellent haul, as this wonderful route takes in no fewer than six peaks above the critical height. All these attractions, not forgetting the enormity and majesty of the views, combine to make this great high-altitude expedition a must for Pyrenean mountaineers.

TROUMOUSE RIDGE

From the car park, head towards the 'Vierge de Troumouse', but turn right after the stream on to the path that contours round the Lacs des Aires (heading south, then east, then north). When below the large grey slabs under the Col de la Sède, follow the faint but cairned path up the rocky and grassy slope to the pass.

Head south along the ridge to the foot of Pic de Gerbats, then go down the Troumouse side for about 50m to a large cairn on a small ridge (II, exposed). Traverse horizontally for about 100m (II, exposed), then head diagonally upwards to regain the crest of the ridge just after the summit. From here it is possible to do the round trip to the summit of Pic de Gerbats by following a wide ledge northwards, then north-westwards.

PIC DE LA MUNIA
TROUMOUSE RIDGE

The view from the summit.

Going up to Pic Heid. On the left, the vertiginous cliffs of the Baroude.

CIRQUE DE TROUMOUSE

Total concentration is needed on the narrowest sections.

Continue easily along the ridge to Pic Heid. The next section of the ridge is narrower but not difficult (II). Continue to the trig point on the summit of Pic de Troumouse. Easy ground leads to the foot of Pic de Serre Mourène. The climb to this summit looks intimidating, but it is not difficult. Climb the crest of the ridge (III+, then III), then continue easily to Pic de la Munia.

DESCENT
Scramble easily down the west ridge to a step. Descend a gully on the left to a small terrace, then climb down the short, cracked and very polished slab of the Pas du Chat (II). From the bottom of the Pas du Chat, go down a gully on the south face for 25m, then turn right to follow a ledge on to the crest of the ridge. Descend easily to the Col de la Munia. Continue northwards, then north-eastwards down easy slopes to get to a tunnel that leads to the lower slopes. Go down a short but very polished step (II, one peg), then follow the cairns north eastwards along the foot of the cliff (beware of stone fall) to a gully that leads to the foot of the face. Head west down a faint path across the scree to get to the grass below. Follow the wide track back to the car park.

GRAND ASTAZOU (3,071m)

OUBLIÉ COULOIR
START POINT: bivouac in the Estaubé Valley or the Espuguettes Hut.
DIFFICULTY: AD+. Grade-II ice. The descent is long and can be exhausting if the snow is soft.
TIMES: 3-4 hrs for the climb.
VERTICAL HEIGHT: 500m
CONDITIONS: December to May, depending on conditions.
GEAR: ice axes, three or four ice screws, two or three pegs, a few small cams and slings.
FIRST ASCENT: B. Lajus and F. Thibaudeau, June 1972.

The most famous gully in the Astazous, even among our Spanish neighbours, is the Swan Couloir. When filled with snow, it has been said to resemble a 'giant bum crack' on the edge of the Cirque de Gavarnie, but it is on every self-respecting Pyrenean mountaineer's hit list and is one of the chain's best snow climbs. Of course, popularity has its downsides and on spring weekends, when conditions are optimal, the Swan Couloir is often packed with climbers, making the ascent much more difficult than it should be. At the same time, hidden on the other side of the summit, the very aptly named Oublié Couloir (*oublié* is French for forgotten) will often remain untrodden. Perhaps the reason this excellent climb is so frequently overlooked is because most people are attracted to places they can see and this corner of the Pyrenees is hidden from view. This is a shame for those who miss out, as this slender thread of snow on the vast north-east face of the Grand Astazou has a lot to offer. The couloir's zigzag path adds interest to the route, as the successive facets of the climb are revealed only one by one as you scale the natural succession of slopes, guided by occasional glimpses of the summit. What is more, the need to continually seek out the correct line is an excellent counter to the sometimes-dangerous feeling of routine that can set in during long snow climbs. The crux of the route, a bottleneck after approximately 150 metres, can be seen from below. It is essential to check that there is plenty of ice on this section before setting off. In addition, it is usually necessary to start the walk-in before dawn because the upper slopes face east and get the sun very early in the morning.

After the excitement and satisfaction of the climb, topping out on the summit often feels like emerging into another world. Monte Perdido is laid out in front of you as a reward for passing the test, its huge north face dominating the horizon. Your trained eye will have no problem picking out the direct route to the summit – a fantastic objective for the next day, but first you can look forward to a relaxing evening at the tiny Tuquerouye hut.

OUBLIÉ COULOIR
From the Espuguettes hut or a bivouac in the Estaubé valley, follow the ski route marked on the IGN map to the foot of the Grand Astazou. The couloir starts at around 2,550m, just to the east of the Hourquette de Pailla. Climb a 40° snow slope to get to the couloir, which steepens to 45° and then 50°. Belay below the bottleneck at 2,710m, which forms the crux of the route (60/70°). It is essential to check whether or not this wall of ice, which can be seen clearly from below, is in condition before starting the route. Climb the wall of ice to a belay on the left bank of the couloir. Continue up the couloir (55°, then 45°), zigzagging up to the foot of a Y-gully at around 2,915m. The left-hand branch leads to the east ridge. Follow the right-hand branch to a rocky buttress, then traverse right (40m) and climb an east-facing gully to gain the ridge (at around 3,000m) above the Hourquette de Pailla. Gain the summit of the Astazou via the north face (55°, then 50°).

DESCENT
Go down the west ridge to the Col Swan, then head south-east to get to Ibón de Marboré. Go up to the Brèche de Tuquerouye and the hut. Descend the north couloir (35/40°) to a small saddle on the left bank (2431m). From here, head easily north-westwards to the bivouac site or the Espuguettes hut.

GAVARNIE

On the upper slopes.

PETIT ASTAZOU (3,012m)

NORTH-WEST RIDGE
START POINT: Espuguettes Hut (2,027m).
DIFFICULTY: AD+. At the beginning of the season, it is important to check conditions on the descent via the Rochers Blancs. Ask the guides office or hut warden.
TIMES: approach 2 hrs; climb 4–5 hrs; descent 3–4 hrs, depending on the option chosen.
VERTICAL HEIGHT: 500m.
CONDITIONS: from spring to autumn.
GEAR: rope, a few nuts and cams, slings, quickdraws. Crampons may be needed for the descent at the beginning of the season and for the climb at the end of the season. A few *in situ* pegs.
FIRST ASCENT: H. Brulle, R. d'Astorg, C. Passet and H. Courtade, 1892.

The Pics d'Astazou are wonderful mountains. Seen from the valley, they look a little stumpy and they are less impressively vertical than the cliffs of Gavarnie, but they house some excellent climbs and their positions on the very edge of the cirque, below the north faces of Pic du Marboré and Monte Perdido, make them exceptional viewpoints. One of the most enjoyable ways of reaching these belvederes is the north-west ridge of the Petit Astazou.

Your experience as a mountaineer will have told you to check out the route past Pic Rouge de Pailla the previous afternoon, because you have to do the first part of the approach in the dark after a pre-dawn start from the Espuguettes hut. Although the Glacier du Pailla is tiny, crampons are often needed to get to the saddle from where the ridge soars elegantly upwards to the summit of the Petit Astazou, 500m higher. Another sharp ridge then leads to the Grand Pic, at 3,071m.

GAVARNIE

The route more-or-less follows the line of the ridge, never straying far from the crest. As always at Gavarnie, the rock is quite unusual, and its blocky, flaky appearance can take a little getting used to. Route finding on this type of ground is always engrossing, while the need to place nuts, cams and slings adds further interest. For seconds, this wonderful day's climbing offers the pleasure of moving over moderately difficult terrain while soaking up the outstanding views, which gradually open out across the high but undistinguished summit of Pic du Marboré to the neighbouring Cilindro de Marboré and Monte Perdido. The huge, upended fold that forms the Cilindro is so imposing it almost overshadows the monarch of the area, which stands proud above its glacial apron, one of the chain's last great glaciers. At its foot lies the lake of Ibón de Marboré, a splash of blue among the yellow folded rocks of the surrounding cliffs.

NORTH-WEST RIDGE

The ridge consists of a dozen steps and the belays are mostly very spacious. Start by climbing three pitches on the ridge crest (II/III). The next step is steeper and is climbed on the left (III+). Continue up a slab to the right of the crest (III+), then climb a smooth-looking wall to get to the top of the fourth step (B6). Follow the right-hand edge of the ridge to a large ledge (III+). Go straight up the next two steps (four pitches) to the foot of a large pedestal (B11). Traverse left along a horizontal crack for about 10m, then climb a slab and go right round a bulge (IV). Continue up the crest to a good platform. Climb diagonally leftwards for about 20m to go round a steep step. Regain the ridge crest via a loose chimney (III+). Follow the crest of the ridge, or its left flank, to overcome two more short walls (III+). Less steep ground leads to the summit.

The Petit Astazou and Glacier du Pailla.

DESCENT

There are two ways of getting down from the route. When there is a lot of snow, it is best to descend the steep slope below the Brèche de Tuquerouye (crampons may be needed) and then go over the Hourquette d'Alans to get back to the hut and Gavarnie. Later in the season, when most of the snow has melted, it is possible to descend via the Col d'Astazou. Go down the west-facing slopes below the col and then head north, past the Rochers Blancs and the Cabane de Pailla. This descent is quite difficult and should not be attempted by inexperienced mountaineers or in bad weather, as it is very easy to get off route, despite the occasional cairns and waymarkers.

Left: Care is required with the unusual rock of the Astazou.

PIC DU MARBORÉ (3,248m)

PASSET RIDGE

START POINT: Sarradets Hut or Cabane du Pailla.
DIFFICULTY: AD+. Long approach, exposed if you traverse the cirque.
TIMES: approx. 3 hrs to traverse the cirque; 3 hrs from the foot of the route to the summit.
VERTICAL HEIGHT: 450m for the ridge.
CONDITIONS: from spring to autumn.
GEAR: 50m rope, a few nuts and cams, slings, crampons and ice axe at the beginning of the season.
FIRST ASCENT: R. Chevalier, J. and R. Mailly, 1938.

For a large part of the nineteenth century, the members of Gavarnie's Passet family seem to have envisaged just one course in life: becoming a mountain guide. Henri and Célestin were happy to follow in the footsteps of their forebears, Hippolyte and Laurent, and they all made their mark on the history of Pyrenean mountaineering. Of the four, it was Célestin who had the most impressive career, acquiring a reputation that spread far beyond the Pyrenees. His exploits included the first one-day ascent of the Meije, climbed with the famous Gaspard, and the fourth ascent of the Drus, which was also the first ascent in one day from Chamonix. However, it was in his native ranges that he accomplished his greatest achievement when he made the first ascent of the Gaube Couloir on the Vignemale, climbed by cutting 1,300 steps.

Fittingly, one of the great ridges on Pic du Marboré, the centrepiece and highest point of the Cirque de Gavarnie, now bears the name of this illustrious mountaineering family. The Passet Ridge is a magnificent climb in the middle of the Pyrenees' most beautiful arena, but the long and exposed approach over difficult terrain makes it a demanding day out.

Moving back on to the ridge crest (pitch 8).

GAVARNIE

On pitch 10 (III+)

PIC DU MARBORÉ
PASSET RIDGE

My favourite way of getting to the ridge is by traversing the cirque from the Sarradets hut, as the trail goes through one of those rare places where the scenery is so overwhelming it makes you feel like an insignificant being crawling through an infinite landscape. However, this approach can only be recommended when the cirque is snow free because sections of the route follow exposed ledges between precipitous slopes. By the time you get to the start of the climb, at the Brèche Passet, the most challenging obstacles are behind you, so you can relax and enjoy, almost nonchalantly, the lovely ascent to the top of the Marboré. The climb itself follows an ingenious line, seeking out the mountain's weaknesses and cleverly avoiding any excessive difficulties. The descent follows the west ridge towards the Brèche de Roland, adding an extra crop of magnificent views and ensuring wonderful memories for many years to come.

APPROACH
There are three options for the approach:

1. From the Sarradets hut, contour eastwards across the scree then traverse a yellow cliff by following a series of ledges (cairns). Continue contouring across unpleasant scree to the left-hand foot of the north face of La Tour. Aim for the ledge between the lower band of yellow rock and the upper band of grey rock. Follow this ledge across the cirque (exposed). Go up slightly to the moraine below the Col de la Cascade, then contour round to the foot of the couloir below the Brèche Passet (3 hrs).

2. If there is too much snow to traverse in from the Sarradets hut, go over the Brèche de Roland and traverse across the Spanish side of the ridge to the Col de la Cascade. From the col, descend into the cirque and then go back up to the Brèche Passet (4 hrs).

3. From the Pailla bivouac hut, go past the Rochers Blancs to the western side of the Glacier du Marboré. Head south up the glacier to a gully that leads to the Brèche Passet (4 hrs).

Looking across the top of the ridge to La Tour, Le Casque and Le Taillon.

PASSET RIDGE
P1: make a gently descending traverse from the Brèche Passet to get to the edge of a wide, red chimney. Climb the right bank of this chimney (40m, III).
P2: traverse right along easy ledges, then continue up the crest to a step in the ridge (40m, II+).
P3: continue up the crest, then move on to the south side of the ridge and climb a chimney. Climb a wall, then continue easily along the crest (50m, III+).
P4: follow the ridge crest (45m, II).

GAVARNIE

P5: follow the ridge crest (40m, III).
P6: follow the ridge crest to gain the foot of a large gendarme at a ledge that leads on to the north face (40m, II).
P7: do not continue along the ledge or head towards the *in situ* pegs. Instead, climb a corner for about 5m to a light-coloured slab. Traverse across the slab, then step down to a small platform (20m, III).
P8: move on to the south side of the ridge by traversing a steep wall, then climb a rightward-leaning crack to get back on to the crest (45m, IV).
P9: follow the ridge to the foot of an overhanging gendarme (50m, II).
P10: descend the south flank of the ridge, go along some ledges, then move back on to the crest at the foot of a couloir (45m, III+). Continue up the couloir, then follow a wide ledge on the south flank of the ridge until it is possible to move back on to the ridge crest. Go up the crest (II). Go right round a wall of dark-coloured rock, then climb a gully to get to a plateau to the right of the summit.

MONTE PERDIDO (3,355m) AND ORDESA VALLEY

NORMAL ROUTE AND TOUR OF THE VALLEY

START POINT: La Pradera car park.
DIFFICULTY: PD with an exposed via ferrata and short sections of climbing. Some steep snow slopes at the beginning of the season. Navigation difficult in bad weather.
TIMES: three days.
VERTICAL HEIGHT: 1,500m (Day 1); 1,100m (Day 2); -1,800m (Day 3).
CONDITIONS: from June to October
GEAR: slings and karabiners, 30m rope, crampons and ice axe at the beginning of the summer.
FIRST ASCENT: Monte Perdido: Rondo, Laurens and a shepherd from Aragon, 1802.

A long, long time ago, the immense Tethys Ocean covered a large part of the Earth, separating two huge continents, Gondwana and Laurasia. Plate-tectonic forces gradually moved these two continents together, closing the Tethys Ocean and initiating a major episode of mountain building known as the Hercynian orogeny (360 to 280 million years ago). In the western part of this tectonic belt, powerful rivers washed debris from the newly emerging chain of mountains into another ancient sea, leading to the accumulation of thick layers of sediment over many millions of years. These sediments were slowly compacted into rock before they were once again pushed skywards by the immense tectonic forces generated when the Iberian and European plates collided between 53 and 33 million years ago. Thus, the shells and fossils found in the limestones of Monte Perdido are of marine origin, a fact that was first demonstrated by Ramond de Carbonnières in 1797. During the Ice Age, glaciers carved these relatively soft and friable rocks into the magnificent landscape we see today and whose uniqueness was recognised by UNESCO in 1997 when the entire area from Gavarnie to Monte Perdido was listed as a World Heritage site.

Gavarnie's north-facing slopes are bleak and harsh, as if tempered by the cold, whereas the southern side of the divide has been carved into immense, sun-kissed canyons that look as if they are attempting to escape from the mountains. The Ordesa Valley, an immense ravine lined with multi-tiered cliffs split by spectacular shelves, is undoubtedly one of the most beautiful areas of the Pyrenees. It is also unusual because, unlike most of the valleys in the Pyrenees, it runs east–west, rather than north–south. Every summer, thousands of hikers flock to the valley, most of whom are channelled along a selection of well-defined routes by the national park's wardens.

Left: The village of Torla.   **Above:** On the famous 'clavijas'.

MONTE PERDIDO

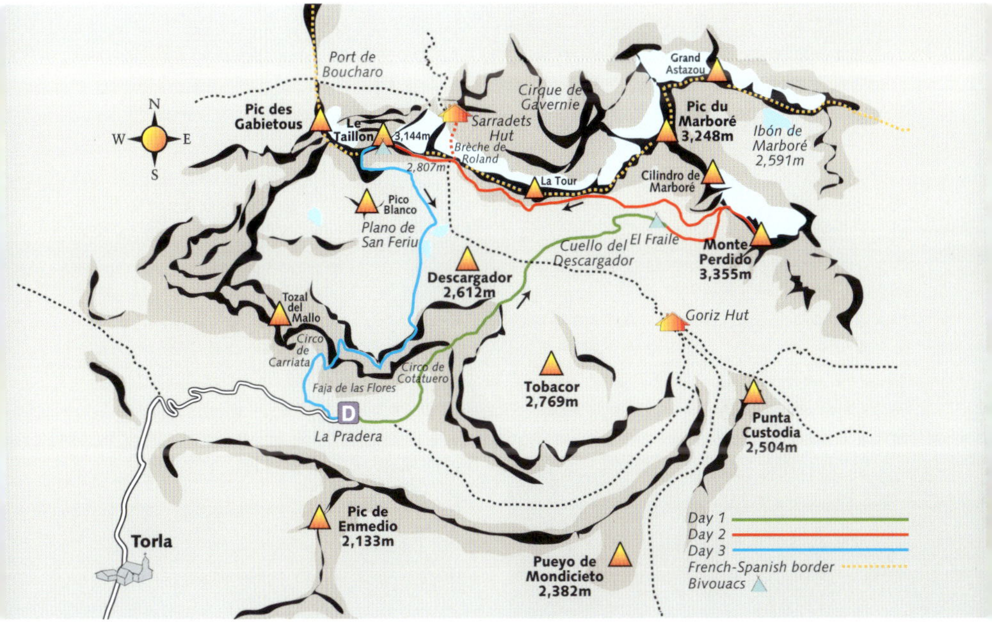

The view across the Ordesa Valley from the 'Hunters' Trail'.

MONTE PERDIDO AND ORDESA VALLEY
NORMAL ROUTE AND TOUR OF THE VALLEY

However, it is still possible to get off the beaten track and enjoy these wonderful mountains away from the crowds.

One of the easiest ways of climbing from the valley floor to the upper terraces is via the Cotatuero ladders, a series of metal rungs that were first installed in 1881 by a blacksmith from Torla at the request of an English hunter. The addition of steel cables has transformed the route into an airy but reassuring via ferrata. In good weather, experienced mountaineers should find the Cotatuero ladders the only real obstacle on the normal route to Monte Perdido, although navigating through the labyrinth of cliffs and ledges can be very difficult if cloud or fog reduces the visibility. Another potential problem is finding drinking water because the rock forming these mountains is extremely porous and as full of holes as Swiss cheese, so any rain immediately percolates into the ground. The locations of springs and streams vary according to the time of year and how much snow there is, so the positions of the bivouac sites described here should be considered approximate locations. In addition, this three-day circuit can be varied in numerous ways, depending on your fitness and how much time you have to explore the innumerable nooks and crannies that make up this delightful valley.

NORMAL ROUTE AND TOUR OF THE VALLEY
Day 1

Follow the track eastwards from the La Pradera car park, then bear left (north-east) on to the path to the Cotatuero ladders (clavijas). Climb the steel rungs up the initial chimney (II+), then follow the via ferrata rightwards across the cliff. Head north-east up the valley. From the upper part of the valley, follow the cairns eastwards above the cliffs. Continue due north over flat

Above: Traversing across the Cotatuero ladders.
Main: Going up to Monte Perdido, looking back to the Cilindro de Marboré and Ibón Helado.

MONTE PERDIDO

Le Casque seen from near the Brèche de Roland.

ground, then head up and diagonally right (north-east) to the Collado del Descargador. Contour round eastwards, then go up diagonally leftwards for several hundred metres to the foot of a cliff. Climb the easiest line up the cliff to get to the wide shelf at Rincón del Fraile, at around 2,800m. It is possible to camp here.
Height gain: 1,500m, 8 hrs.

Day 2
Contour round eastwards to the Monte Perdido path. Go up steeper ground to Ibón Helado, where you can leave your sacks to do the round trip to the summit of Monte Perdido. Start by going up a spur, then follow the valley to the summit (snow at the beginning of the season). Go back down to Ibón Helado, then, at around 2,900m, go along a horizontal ledge to the south of the Cilindro de Marboré to get to the large cirque below Pic du Marboré. Descend slightly to a wide ledge that is followed westwards along the base of the cliff below the Pics de la Cascade. This takes you almost to L'Epaule, after which it is possible to go back up on to the frontier ridge, from where there is a magnificent bird's-eye view of the Cirque de Gavarnie. Continue heading west to go below La Tour. Climb down a 50m step (II), then continue westwards towards the Col des Isards, at the foot of Le Casque. Do not go down to the col. Instead, traverse along the base of the cliff to a steep section with an *in situ* cable. Continue along the foot of the cliff to the Brèche de Roland. From here it is possible to go down the French side and sleep at the Sarradets hut. If you prefer to bivouac, continue heading west to a bivouac site just below the summit of Le Taillon.
Height gain: 1,100m to Le Taillon, 7 hrs.

Day 3
From the summit of Le Taillon, head south, then south-east to the vast Plano de Millaris, to the west of the Collado de Millaris. Head south across the plateau, then go down a cliff (II+) and continue southwards across another plateau. Head south-west across a vast limestone pavement to get to the Faja de las Flores at around 2,300m. Head west along this magnificent ledge to the Circo de Carriata. Bear left between two cliffs and go down a scree slope towards a cliff. Go down the Carriata ladders ('Clavijas de Salarons', II), then follow the path to the car park at La Pradera.
Height loss: 1,800m, 6 hrs.

MONTE PERDIDO (3,355m)

ESPARRETS SPUR AND EAST RIDGE
START POINT: Tuquerouye Hut or bivouac at Ibón de Marboré.
DIFFICULTY: D+.
TIMES: approx. 8 hrs for the climb.
VERTICAL HEIGHT: 800m for the spur and ridge.
CONDITIONS: from spring to autumn.
GEAR: two 50m ropes, set of nuts, set of cams, a few pegs, slings, crampons, ice axe.
FIRST ASCENT: the Ravier brothers, 1973.

All the faces of Monte Perdido are striking, but its north face is undoubtedly the most spectacular, the biggest, the most emblematic. The hanging glacier – cut in two but still very imposing, the monumental rocky summit and the sheer size of the face force the respect of hikers on the footpaths at its foot. 'What terrible cries must the Earth have vented when giving birth to these mountains … ', wrote one famous author. Could any other words better describe the colossal forces needed to raise these summits towards the heavens?

The shores of Ibón de Marboré, at the foot of the face, are the best place from which to admire this grandiose landscape and to marvel at the incredible folds in the rock of the Cilindro. It is on this plateau, at 2,500m, that you will sleep before your encounter with the Esparrets Spur.

You could, of course, spend the night in the tiny Tuquerouye hut, just a few metres above the lake, if it is not already full. However, the time you save in the morning by bivouacking may well be precious at the end of what will be a very long day. The approach zigzags intelligently through the ledges, guiding you unhesitatingly into the middle of the great east face. Even the climb follows a natural line, so there are few doubts as to which way to go, although the almost total absence of *in situ* gear means the leader still has a lot of work to do. The upper section is more a scramble than a climb, but you are unlikely to meet another soul, unless, as another famous writer believed, 'some places retain in their memories the imprint of all the men who have travelled through them … '

Bold climbing on P5 (IV+).

MONTE PERDIDO

Monte Perdido and the Cilindro de Marboré seen from the north-east.

Above the glacier while descending via the escape route below the summit.

MONTE PERDIDO
ESPARRETS SPUR AND EAST RIDGE

The descent follows the normal route down the north face, so it is worth taking the time the evening before the climb to identify the easiest place to get through the long cliff below the glacier.

ESPARRETS SPUR AND EAST RIDGE

Go to the south-east edge of the plateau, then head diagonally up the scree (cairns) to a horizontal ledge. Follow the cairns eastwards along this ledge. Go under a jammed block to get to a small notch with a bolt. Descend a gully (II) for about 20m, then traverse across its left bank (III) to a parallel gully, which is followed to easier ground. Traverse right, then go up the scree for about 100m to a distinctive black slab at the foot of the spur (1¾ hrs). Start at a chimney to the left of this slab and to the left of a small overhang, 2,560m.

P1: climb the chimney, then head right up a second chimney to gain the crest of the spur (45m, IV+).

• Follow the easier-angled ridge for three pitches to a steep wall (II/III).

P5: climb slightly rightwards to get to a crack, then continue up a slab to the crest of the ridge. Belay at the foot of a chimney (45m, bold IV+, then III/IV).

• Go up the chimney, then climb three more pitches (III+, III, IV) to get to the top of a small needle.

• Abseil (15m) to the notch on the other side of the needle. Go up about 10m to belay at the foot of a corner.

P9: do not climb the corner. Instead, move right and climb another chimney for about 15m. Traverse right again along a small terrace to get to a parallel chimney with a jammed block at about 15m.

Above: The upper section of the ridge, looking down to the Pineta Valley.

Left: Pitch 1 (IV+).

MONTE PERDIDO

Near the ledges at the end of the climbing.

Climb this chimney, then traverse left slightly to follow cracks to belay at the base of a corner (45m, V).
- Climb the corner, then traverse left on to the crest of the ridge, which is followed to a terrace where the angle of the ridge eases (45m, V).
- Climb the crest for one pitch (III).
- Go along a small ledge on the south side of the ridge (III) to get to two deep gullies. Climb the right-hand gully, then move into the left-hand one (III) to get to a series of ledges (5–6 hrs of climbing).
- Traverse across the ledges for about 100m, then go straight up steep slopes split by short steps (II) to get to the ridge that leads to the eastern saddle.
- From the saddle, move left below a vertical wall. Climb the cliff, first diagonally leftwards, then diagonally rightwards (III/III+).
- Wide, east-facing slopes lead easily to the summit.

DESCENT
Go down the couloir in the north-west face, above Ibón Helado, then head north to the Cuello del Cilindro. Go down the scree below the col to the glacier. At the foot of the glacier, traverse east for about 200m, then follow cairns northwards and go down through the cliff (II+). Head down the moraine on the left towards Ibón Helado.

At the end of the climbing, it is possible to descend without going to the summit by heading west along the terraces to the northern glacier. Cross the glacier (beware of crevasses) to join the descent route below it.

THE VIGNEMALE

'You adopt a mountain, you marry it, you adore it, you present it proudly to your friends, and you end up attributing it many virtues and much beauty, idealising it to such an extent that you no longer have eyes, no longer have love for any but her. I got like that with the Vignemale.'

The man who wrote this short confession was, of course, Henry Russell, the nineteenth-century English count, great eccentric and indefatigable explorer whose name is intrinsically intertwined with the history of this celebrated mountain. Russell was a fervent romanticist who loved nature and the great outdoors, and who was happiest in wilderness areas. However, he differed from many of his contemporaries in that he did not actively seek out the pleasures of hard living. He spent a large part of his life travelling and visited many different lands across the globe before deciding that, for him, the Pyrenees were the most beautiful mountains in the world. His attachment to the Vignemale was particularly intense. In fact, history may never have seen another love affair between a man and a mountain that was so profound, so undying and so passionate.

After claiming the first two summer ascents of the Vignemale, in 1861 and 1868, he did the third ascent of the mountain in the winter of 1869, which made it the first major winter ascent in Europe. In 1889, he signed a contract with the government authorities to rent the entire mountain for ninety-nine years, thereby tying his life to this most alpine of Pyrenean peaks. He had caves dug into the mountainside so he would have comfortable quarters near the summit where he and his more adventurous guests could enjoy what were sometimes very festive nights. His fascination with the mountain led him to spend weeks on end observing the movements of its glacier, listening to the long silences and terrifying sounds of nature, and gazing into the profound darkness of summer nights.

While Russell was preoccupied with these more contemplative pursuits, other people were setting themselves more ambitious challenges on the other side of the mountain. For example, Henri Brulle and Jean Bazillac, who had introduced technical climbing to the Pyrenees in 1879 with their ascent of the Clot de la Hount Couloir, decided to attempt the much more difficult Gaube Couloir. Accompanied by Roger de Monts and François Bernat-Salles, they achieved their goal thanks to the efforts of the great guide Célestin Passet, who had to cut no fewer than 1,300 steps in the snow and ice of the north face. This audacious climb, accomplished in 1889, was so far ahead of its time that it did not receive a second ascent until 1933, forty-four years later. On learning of this feat, Russell somewhat bitterly and scornfully retorted, 'next time, it will have to be climbed facing backwards'. But Russell's dismissive comment could not disguise the fact that the days of hard climbing had come.

Since then, around twenty routes, on both rock and ice, have been climbed on the north faces of the massif's summits. The easiest are described here. They are all excellent climbs that will delight every mountaineer, whether they are the pinnacle of your climbing career or mere springboards to more ambitious challenges. And one thing is certain, their first ascent of this magnificent peak forever retains a special place in the hearts of everyone who climbs the Vignemale.

VIGNEMALE (3,298m)

PETIT VIGNEMALE-PIQUE LONGUE RIDGE
START POINT: Oulettes Hut.
DIFFICULTY: PD. Rock climb along the crest of the ridge. Sections of grade III (including two on the descent), difficult to protect.
TIMES: 2½ hrs from the Petit Vignemale to Pique Longue.
VERTICAL HEIGHT: 300m
CONDITIONS: from spring to autumn.
GEAR: a few nuts and cams, karabiners and slings.
FIRST ASCENT: unknown.

Most of the hikers who reach the summit of the Petit Vignemale are content to quietly savour their exploit, wishing only to contemplate the surrounding mountains and valleys from the top of this 3,000m peak. However, there are others who appear a little dissatisfied, disappointed even, that they found the climb so easy, and who have already started wondering whether they should have set themselves a tougher challenge. In this they are akin to those people, found in all the world's ports, who are intimidated by the ocean but who gaze longingly out to sea, vowing that one day they will set sail. On the Petit Vignemale, such people tend to stare across at the ridge leading to Pique Longue, watching any climbers they see with the same envy the shore-bound feel for sailors heading off on a long voyage.

Looking back from the Petit Vignemale to the Glacier d'Ossoue and the Montferrat.

VIGNEMALE MASSIF

Some of them will return to the Vignemale with a new dream and different gear, and take their first steps along this little ridge and into the world of mountaineering. If climbs were classified according to how enjoyable they are, the traverse from the Petit Vignemale to its big brother would be very high on the list for two main reasons. First, it is easy enough to appeal to novice mountaineers, who, I believe, have a greater capacity for appreciating the wonderfully exposed positions. Second, the ridge is so short and its difficulties are overcome so quickly that you will have the time and the energy to get the most from each section of the route and to enjoy every moment of the climb, without a single second in which to feel bored. The brevity of the ridge is also likely to leave novices hungry for more, whetting their appetite to repeat the experience on other routes as soon as they can.

PETIT VIGNEMALE-PIQUE LONGUE RIDGE

Go down the first step below the top of the Petit Vignemale to a muddy saddle. Follow the ridge for about 20m, then climb down its south side to another saddle with an abseil station (III). Climb or abseil down the north side of the saddle, first going straight down and then heading westwards (25m, III) to get back on to the ridge. Follow the ridge crest to the foot of the Aiguille des Glaciers (II). Climb the south flank of the ridge (II+/III), then continue easily to the top of the Aiguille. Continue to the Pointe Chausenque, then descend diagonally across its south face to the glacier. Follow the normal route to the summit of Pique Longue.

PETIT VIGNEMALE (3,032m)

NORTH SPUR
START POINT: Oulettes Hut or Baysselance Hut.
DIFFICULTY: D-.
TIMES: approx. 4½ hrs from the foot of the spur to the summit.
VERTICAL HEIGHT: 350m.
CONDITIONS: from spring to autumn.
GEAR: a few nuts and cams, slings.
FIRST ASCENT: R. Cazenave, H. Paradis, C. Cornélius and A. Subot, 1947.

Nestled comfortably in the shadow of its big brother, the Petit Vignemale is the last summit on the ridge below Pique Longue. This is undoubtedly the Pyrenees' most accessible 3,000-metre peak, as the presence of the Baysselance hut at the foot of the mountain means hikers can reach the summit in little more than an hour by following the very straightforward normal route. However, this is the only easy way to climb the Petit Vignemale, as its other faces are much more abrupt. To the south, the mountainside plunges straight down to the Glacier d'Ossoue in a smooth and intimidating precipice that reflects off the surface of the ice. To the north, the spur is bounded by the Glacier du Petit Vignemale, which boasts some of the last séracs in the Pyrenees. How much longer will they last?

The proximity of the glacier gives the North Spur a very forbidding character that belies the relatively uncommitting nature of the climbing. In addition, it includes a unique series of features for a rock climb in these mountains, offering a combination of exposed slabs, elegant ridges and clean-cut chimneys. As everywhere on the north face, the very compact rock provides few cracks in which to place nuts or cams, which can make the climbing quite intimidating. This is especially the case on pitches 4 and 5, despite the relatively easy climbing, as the rare pegs and bolts are difficult to see, and natural protection is hard to find. However, the best climbing is on the upper pitches, where the route follows the crest of the spur, high above the huge crevasses that split the surface of the glacier – suddenly, it is difficult to tear your eyes from the magnificent surroundings and concentrate on the climbing. The final section of the route is much easier, as the face lies back, opening the way to the summit of this great mountain.

Pitch 7.

VIGNEMALE MASSIF

APPROACH
1. From Les Oulettes, follow the Hourquette d'Ossoue path, turning off just before the pass to traverse across to the route (1½ hrs).

2. From the Baysselance hut, go over the Hourquette and descend the Les Oulettes side for about 70m, then traverse across to the route (40 mins).

NORTH SPUR
Go up the glacier to reach the spur just to the right of its lowest point, at the foot of a leftward-trending ramp.

P1: climb the ramp to a large ledge (50m, III+).
P2: continue along the ramp for 20m to the foot of a steep wall (possible belay). Climb the wall, first on the left, then via a corner. Traverse 15m right to belay below a dyke of green ophite (45m, IV+).
P3: climb this dyke (45m, IV, then III).
P4: continue up the dyke for 15m. When it becomes easy, traverse right for 10m, then go straight up the slabs above (bold). Belay at the start of a short crack (45m, III, two pegs).
P5: continue straight up the slabs to belay on a rightward-slanting ledge, approx. 6m from the crest of the spur (45m, III).
P6: go straight up for 10m, then traverse right to a chimney-crack that leads to a notch on the crest, above a gendarme (20m, III).
P7: traverse right for 10m (on the séracs side of the ridge), then go up a smooth wall to the crest of the ridge. Belay to the right of the crest, at the start of a crack (35m, III+).
P8: climb the crack and a yellow chimney, then move back on to the crest (40m, III).
P9: continue up the crest to a subsidiary summit before a small saddle (35m, III).

The upper part of the ridge lies back. Follow it for about 100m to the foot of a scree-filled gully (II). Go up the leftward-trending gully, then move on to its right bank to get to the summit (II+).

VIGNEMALE (3,298M)

CLASSIC NORTH FACE ROUTE
START POINT: Oulettes Hut.
DIFFICULTY: D+.
TIMES: approach 2 hrs; climb 7–8 hrs.
VERTICAL HEIGHT: approx. 850m.
CONDITIONS: as soon as the face is dry.
GEAR: two 50m ropes, set of nuts, set of cams, slings, a few pegs, crampons.
FIRST ASCENT: H. Barrio and R. Bellocq, 1933.

On the long traverse at the foot of the red schist.

The north face of the Vignemale, an enormous bastion rising almost a thousand metres above the séracs of the contorted Glacier des Oulettes, is undoubtedly the most 'alpine' face in the Pyrenees. It is on this immense wall, striated by steep and forbidding gullies, that some of the greatest pages in the history of Pyrenean mountaineering have been written. Just above the bergschrund at the foot of the Gaube Couloir, a thread of green serpentine marks the start of one of the face's best climbs. Those setting off on this adventure cannot help but feel a tremor of excitement as they cross the bergschrund in the cold light of dawn. This is often where climbers make their first acquaintance with the face, as the Classic North Face Route is the easiest climb on Pique Longue, with moves that are never harder than grade V. Nevertheless, solid technical skills and experience are needed to ensure success and many people would be proud to crown their mountaineering achievements with this superb climb. It is also an excellent test of a climber's ability to seek out the best line and to climb efficiently and steadily while making technical moves high above protection placed in rock of doubtful solidity. As such, it is a good route on which to assess your skills before attempting more ambitious projects. Such tests may be exacting, but they are essential and formative stages in every mountaineer's career.

Once committed on the route, retreat is almost impossible and there are no ways off the face until you get to the Gaube Ridge. Here, teams who no longer have the time or energy to continue to the summit can slink off down to the valley without having to climb the final bastion.

VIGNEMALE MASSIF

Those who do make it to the top can enjoy a few moments of peaceful reflection before heading back to the hut, either via the glacier or, better still, by descending the elegant ridge over the Petit Vignemale and thereby prolonging the joys of this great mountaineering adventure.

CLASSIC NORTH FACE ROUTE

Climb a pitch up the serpentine dyke (V). Move right and climb a chimney to a platform (40m, V). If it is impossible to cross the bergschrund directly below the serpentine dyke, descend for 100m, then go up some rightwards-sloping ledges to get to a corner on the left that can be climbed to the platform (two pitches, V). Continue more easily for 150m (II/III), then climb a series of small steps towards the large gully on the edge of the intermediary ridge (100m, III). Before getting to the gully, head left for 20m along the ledge that leads to the foot of the intermediary ridge. Descend towards a hollow (III+) to the left of the ridge, then go back up on to the ridge near a small notch, beside a gendarme (50m, III). Continue up the ridge to a vertical orange wall. Go down leftwards for 3m, then climb an ochre-coloured chimney to get back on the ridge (IV). The wall can also be climbed directly (6a or A0). Climb an overhanging, cracked wall (40m, IV+), then continue more easily up the ridge. Move right slightly and follow a small corner (III+) to a large ledge, then head back left to gain the summit of the intermediary ridge (III+). Traverse left for about 100m, going up slightly to gain a small notch at the foot of a well-marked spur of red schist. Go up this spur, first slightly leftwards, then straight up (50m, III), to a steep, light coloured wall. Climb this wall (IV), then traverse more easily for 20m to belay at the start of a ledge that leads rightwards to the Gaube Ridge (40m, IV). From the Gaube Ridge, bear left to go straight up the buttress and then move left to avoid an overhang (IV). Move back right along a crack (III+) and ledges, then go straight up to the summit (sections of IV).

VIGNEMALE
CLASSIC NORTH FACE ROUTE

DESCENTS

1. Via the glacier: descend a rocky slope southwards to get to the glacier. Go down its right bank, then traverse north-east to get to the path to the Baysselance hut. Follow the GR10 to Les Oulettes (3 hrs).

2. Via the ridge to the Petit Vignemale: descend to the glacier and go down its left bank to a ledge that can be traversed easily to the shoulder below the Pointe Chausenque. Go down the ridge to the Col des Glaciers, staying mostly on the south side (II, III). Traverse across the pass on to

VIGNEMALE MASSIF

A ray of sun illuminates the glacier at the foot of the route.

the Les Oulettes side and follow a small gully on to the crest of the ridge (III). Climb a steep wall (III+), and follow the ridge to the Petit Vignemale. Head eastwards down the normal route to the Hourquette d'Ossoue.

3. Via the Gaube Ridge: mostly used as an escape route if it is too late to continue to the summit. Follow the crest of the ridge northwards to the Col des Oulettes, from where a good path (a few moves of III+) leads back to the hut.

THE BALAÏTOUS

In 1864, a young English lawyer and accomplished mountaineer called Charles Packe set off to climb the Balaïtous. His excitement and enthusiasm at the prospect of making the first ascent were still intact, even though this would be his second attempt on this virgin peak. 'There's the enemy that awaits us', exclaimed his guide when they got within sight of the mountain. A few hours later, exhausted but indescribably happy, the two men reached their long-desired goal. However, their great joy, the heady euphoria of claiming a much sought-after prize, was short-lived. A few seconds after getting to the top, they were stupefied to find the remains of a building and a few wooden stakes. 'Tent pegs, most surely.' Obviously, someone had been there before them, but who? No one from the surrounding valleys or the very small circle of mid-nineteenth-century mountaineers was able to throw light on an enigma worthy of the best detective novels.

It was not until 1898 that the identities of the first ascenionists were revealed, thanks to a fortuitous discovery by the historian Henri Béraldi. While working on his magnum opus *Cent ans aux Pyrénées* ('One Hundred Years in the Pyrenees'), Béraldi came upon some storage boxes from the 1820s containing reports filed by two government surveyors, Lieutenants Peytier and Hossard. It was these two surveyors who had made the unheralded first ascent of the Balaïtous in 1825, thirty-nine years before Packe. But this was not the only surprise revealed by these reports – Peytier and Hossard did not make the first ascent of the Balaïtous alone; they were accompanied by a whole group of mapmakers, workers and porters, who stayed on the summit for several days.

The same group also made the second ascent, an expedition that turned into a true epic. Towards the end of August the following year, at the end of a difficult climb, the happy band once again reached the summit and set up camp. Unfortunately, the weather turned the very next day and the surveying team was battered by the full fury of the elements. They were spared nothing: high winds, freezing temperatures and thick snow. After seven days of these extreme conditions and with no hope of provisions arriving, the men finally accepted that they would have to go down. They had run out of food and had already spent almost thirty-six hours without eating. Retreat was difficult and dangerous, but they had no choice. A few days later, the two surveyors went back up to finish taking their measurements and recover the equipment they had abandoned, but only one member of the original group would go with them.

The most surprising aspect of this story is that three expeditions, during which at least twenty men had spent several days on a difficult and previously unclimbed summit, could have been so comprehensively forgotten in so short a time. The tent pegs Peytier and Hossard had abandoned caused great amazement when they were found just thirty-nine years later, and a further thirty-four years had to go by before the story behind them finally became known. Even today, when traversing the Béraldi Ledges, the route the first ascensionists are thought to have taken, you have to feel admiration for the conquerors of this 'knot of precipices', as Henry Russell called it. Lying a long way from the nearest inhabited valleys, and surrounded by some of the longest and narrowest ridges in the Pyrenees, the Balaïtous is not a mountain that gives in easily. It is a challenge that is both feared and prized by modern adventurers, whether they follow one of the tortuous normal routes or a more technical itinerary. Strangely, the summit capping the mountain's highly ravined flanks is completely flat, as if tamed, allowing you to relax and enjoy the serenity of the surroundings to the full. Perhaps already dreaming of other worlds ...

The ledge below the Flammes de Pierre on the Balaïtous' Diable Ridge.

BALAÏTOUS (3,144m)

NORTH-WEST RIDGE
START POINT: Larribet Hut.
DIFFICULTY: D.
TIMES: 4–5 hrs for the climb.
VERTICAL HEIGHT: 500m.
CONDITIONS: from spring to autumn.
GEAR: 50m rope, nuts, cams, slings, quickdraws, ice axe and crampons at the beginning of the season.
FIRST ASCENT: H. Lamathe, H. Le Breton and J. Senmartin, 8 August 1932.

Hikers traversing the narrow Grande Diagonale ledge on the Balaïtous normal route occasionally hear voices. Looking across, they see miniscule silhouettes balancing along the crest of a razor-sharp ridge. Some of the climbers edging their way up this arête may have set off from the hut very early with the seemingly crazy idea of linking all three of the Balaïtous's great ridges – the North-West, Costérillou and Diable. This combination is one of the Pyrenees' great granite adventures, although few mountaineers manage to complete all three routes in a single day. The North-West Ridge is the first part of this epic trilogy and a magnificent climb in its own right. Almost 500 metres high and nearly vertical towards the top, it feels more like a face climb than a ridge, perhaps because the route wisely tends to follow the flanks of the crest, thereby reducing the feeling of exposure. What is more, the rock is mostly good and the route has a wonderful atmosphere.

Once at the summit, you can see how far you would still have to climb to get to the Diable Ridge via the Costérillou Ridge, and imagine what it would be like to continue on to the second part of one of the longest challenges in the Pyrenees.

APPROACH
From the hut, follow the H.R.P. (Pyrenees High-Level Route) through the Cirque de Batcrabère to the Lacs de Micoulaou, at 2,300m. Head south-east up the slope to the foot of the ridge (1½–2 hrs).

The ridge can also be reached from the Arrémoulit hut by going over the Col du Palas and Col du Lavedan.

NORTH-WEST RIDGE
From the lakes, go up the Cirque de Laraillé for about 100m, then follow a rightwards-trending ledge to the start of the climb (150m, I/II). Follow the crest of the ridge for two pitches to get to two gendarmes (100m, III+). Follow easy ledges on the right (west) flank of the gendarmes to the foot of the Aiguille Lamathe. Traverse right slightly and climb a chimney. Move into a second chimney parallel to the first (40m, III+), then climb the crack above. A section of white rock leads to a belay in a distinctive niche on the right (40m, IV+). Go straight up and climb a cracked corner (two pegs), exiting left on to the white slabs, which lead to a belay on the crest of the ridge (45m, IV+). Continue up the crest. Go over a small overhang and then climb cracked slabs to get to the top of the Aiguille Lamathe (30m, IV). Either do two short (20m) diagonal abseils or climb down the crest of the ridge to the notch. Climb a short, overhanging wall on the left (IV), then continue along the crest. Follow ledges round the west side of a nose to a small notch. Descend a gully to the west for 10m, then do another traverse to avoid a second gendarme. Go across a gully to a large ledge at the foot of the final step. Climb straight up for one pitch (50m, III+), then head diagonally rightwards to follow a ledge to its end (50m, II+). Climb a wall, then move left along another ledge to the foot of the Fauchay slab (IV). Go straight up the slab (IV+, two pegs), then go across to its right-hand corner to get to easy rocks. Climb these broken rocks, trending slightly right (III) to just before the Brèche des Isards, where the climbing ends. Traverse west, then follow the top part of the Grande Diagonale leftwards.

BALAÏTOUS

DESCENT
There are two possible descent routes:

1. The Grande Diagonale: from the summit, retrace your steps to the Brèche des Isards, then follow a ledge diagonally leftwards (south-west) to a scree slope above the Michaud shelter (one grade-II move). Go down the slope past the shelter, then go over the Col Noir and descend the Cirque de Batcrabère to the Larribet hut (approx. 3 hrs).

 This descent is not advisable if there is snow on the Grande Diagonale.

2. The Béraldi Ledges. At the end of the season it is also possible to descend via these ledges, which start at the Brèche des Isards.

 Traverse across the northern flank of the Balaïtous to the Brèche Peytier Hossard, just above the Glacier de las Néous. Either go down the glacier or go over a small ridge and head north down the Boulevard Packe to the Larribet hut.

The ledge between the two gendarmes.

PÈNE SARRIÈRE (1,944m)

SOUTH RIDGE
START POINT: Gourette.
DIFFICULTY: AD-.
TIMES: approach 1 hr; climb 2 hrs; descent 45 mins.
VERTICAL HEIGHT: approx. 600m from Gourette to the summit.
CONDITIONS: from spring to autumn.
GEAR: slings, a few nuts, six quickdraws.
FIRST ASCENT: F. Cazalet, and H. Sarthou, 1928.

At first sight, the Pène Sarrière appears particularly characterless, a nondescript lump that rises a mere 600 metres above Gourette. However, the grassy, north-facing slope that can be seen from the resort hides a very surprising profile, as the mountain tapers away dramatically to form two huge and compact vertical walls overlooking the Anglas Valley and the ski runs. Local climbers first began exploring these 'mini big walls' in the late 1950s and they now boast several high quality but quite difficult routes. The cliffs of the east and west faces are capped by the South Ridge, a route that has a special place among Pyrenean ridge climbs, not for the beauty of the surroundings or the quality of the rock, but for the thrills and joy it gives to novice mountaineers. The climbing is never very technical and even inexperienced climbers should not have any difficulty overcoming the grade-III moves dotted along the crest. On the other hand, few other ridges in the Pyrenees offer such airy positions as the traverse of this razor-sharp fin of rock. How climbers tackle the ridge will depend on how bold they are feeling and how intimidated they are by the exposure. Some will balance along the crest, like tightrope walkers, others will sit astride the ridge and shuffle along it, testing the toughness of their trousers. The South Ridge is quite short, so there is no need to rush and, whether you are a beginner or an experienced climber, you are sure to have a great time.

Astride the ridge, looking down to the Anglas Valley.

GOURETTE

A slab suspended in the void.

PÈNE SARRIÈRE
SOUTH RIDGE

Approaching the summit above the resort of Gourette.

SOUTH RIDGE
Follow the Cotch chairlift from the resort car park, then go below the west face of the Pène Sarrière. The climb starts at an obvious saddle at the southern end of the ridge. Follow the crest of the ridge – more or less elegantly – for 60m, then climb a slab to get to the top of the first pinnacle (III). Go down a steep wall (10m, III), then continue easily to the foot of the second pinnacle. Climb its eastern edge, then traverse left across a large ledge (III). Follow a chimney to the top of the third pinnacle, after which the ridge is much wider. Descend smooth slabs (II) to the next saddle. Go up 15m to a large ledge (II), then climb the short overhanging wall above (III+). Continue up a gully to the summit.

DESCENT
Follow the path down the grassy slopes of the north face.

GOURETTE

Is it really very easy?

PIC D'AMOULAT (2,594m)

WEST RIDGE

START POINT: Gourette.
DIFFICULTY: D. There is little *in situ* gear and natural protection is hard to place, so climbers must be confident at the grade. The descent is very exposed and requires great care.
TIMES: approach 2½ hrs; climb 2½ hrs; descent 2 hrs.
VERTICAL HEIGHT: 180m.
CONDITIONS: as soon as the route and descent are free of snow.
GEAR: set of nuts, set of cams, a few pegs, slings.
FIRST ASCENT: P. Daudu, J. Mole and R. Ollivier, 1948.

The resort of Gourette is surrounded by beautiful limestone peaks and seemingly impregnable ramparts of smooth, white calcite dominate the view in every direction. To get to these cliffs, there is no choice but to go through the ski resort, so people who are offended by the presence of chairlifts will have to keep their eyes to the ground and do their best to forget their surroundings. But those who manage to ignore the pylons and cables will reap their just reward, as many of the routes on these buttresses are of excellent quality. If the West Ridge of Pic d'Amoulat were a little closer to the road, it would almost certainly have become a great classic, with climbers flocking to enjoy the wonderfully compact but highly featured rock.

Right: The superbly featured rock on pitch 4 (IV).
Below: Pitch 2 follows an open chimney.

GOURETTE

PIC D'AMOULAT
WEST RIDGE

Yet, despite the proximity of the ski runs, it has retained a secluded air, protected from over-popularity by the relatively long approach.

Climbers intending to tackle this route will need to be comfortable at the grade, as the *in situ* gear is widely spaced and the compact limestone provides few opportunities for placing natural protection. Nevertheless, the solid rock and superb surroundings make this a wonderful place to spend a day in the mountains. What is more, the day's challenges continue even after you have reached the summit of this fabulous viewpoint because great care and a sure foot are needed for the descent, especially when traversing the exposed and crumbling ramp that leads back to the Col d'Amoulat. Together, these factors have prevented the West Ridge becoming a well-travelled trade route and helped it retain its unspoilt character. A must for every visiting mountaineer.

APPROACH
From Gourette, go up the ski slopes between Pène Médaa and Pic de Ger to a small cirque at 2,239m. Traverse round the little lakes at Plaa Ségouné to the Col d'Amoulat. Go over the pass and descend the other side for about 50m, following the foot of the cliffs of Pic d'Amoulat. The route starts 40m below a gully bordered by a corner (2½ hrs).

WEST RIDGE
Go up slabs to the foot of the corner on the edge of the gully (B1, 40m, III). Traverse left to climb the polished gully for 15m (bold). Exit left and go up an area of shattered rock to a section of less-steep ground (B2, 40m, IV). Bear right across smooth slabs to belay on a ledge at the foot of a steep wall (B3, 50m, III+). Climb this very steep wall on undercuts (bold), then continue straight up highly featured slabs to a belay on a large thread (B4, V, then IV, 45m). Climb a runnel/crack to another thread, then bear right slightly to climb the superb slabs on the crest of the ridge (B5, 40m, IV+). Go straight up for about 20m, then traverse right below an area of loose rock to belay at a diagonal crack at the foot of a compact but highly featured wall (B6, 40m, III+). Move right slightly and climb a crack to gain easier ground and the summit.

DESCENT
Follow the east ridge for about 50m, then abseil (50m) or climb (III) down the north side. Follow gravel-covered ledges back to the Col d'Amoulat (II) and the approach route.

Left: Just before the summit, looking across to Pic de Ger.
Right: Lovely climbing with superb views of the Pic du Midi d'Ossau.

GOURETTE

PIC DU MIDI D'OSSAU (2,884m)

TRAVERSE OF THE FOUR PEAKS
START POINT: Pombie Hut.
DIFFICULTY: D. Long route with little *in situ* gear.
TIMES: approach 1¼ hrs; climb 8–10 hrs; descent 2 hrs.
VERTICAL HEIGHT: 800m.
CONDITIONS: from spring to autumn.
GEAR: two 50m ropes, set of cams, set of nuts, slings.
FIRST ASCENT: F. Cazalet and J. Santé, 3 September 1933.

The Pic du Midi is such a familiar presence to the people of the Ossau Valley, they sometimes call it Jean-Pierre. Is this just an affectionate nickname for this great mass of rock, as many visitors think? Or is it a result of the mountain's two asymmetrical summits being linked to the local tradition of naming the first-born son Jean and the second son Pierre? Some experts have yet another theory. They will tell you that the sobriquet for the Pic du Midi d'Ossau's twin peaks is actually derived from the old Pyrenean healing ritual of 'passing through the tree', in which two men, referred to as Jean and Pierre, would heal a sick child by passing her or him several times through an oak branch split in two.

No matter the truth of these stories, this great mountain is as impressive from close quarters as it is venerated in the valleys. According to some, it is the remains of an ancient volcanic plug; others maintain it was hewn from a mass of extrusive rocks. As would be expected for such an impregnable-looking fortress, there are no easy ways to scale its steep walls and more than one experienced climber has been led astray by the complex structure of the face. Traversing the four summits is an excellent way of getting a feel for the intricacies of the mountain. The complete traverse is a long and strenuous expedition, although several escape options allow the route to be shortened if necessary. If you keep an eye on the time, especially when you get to the Grand Pic, you will be able to decide whether you are moving quickly enough to complete the traverse or whether you should beat an honourable retreat via the normal route. Without the pressure of having to complete the traverse at all costs, you will have the peace of mind to enjoy the superb views that open up all along the way.

Its length is not the only challenging feature of this superb route, as the climbing is quite strenuous and most of the pitches require placing nuts and friends to back up the widely spaced *in situ* pegs. So, teams hoping to complete the entire traverse will have to be quite fit and, preferably, ready to attempt the climb during the long days around the summer solstice.

TRAVERSE OF THE FOUR PEAKS
From the hut, go up the left-hand side of the Grande Raillère until you can see an area of ledges at the foot of the Pombie-Peyreget Couloir, directly below the notch between Pointe J. Santé and Pointe d'Aragon. Traverse right to these ledges and follow them to a short wall just below a large orange slab.

Climb the short wall (III), then head right up the ledge to the base of the gully (50m). Go up the gully for about 10m, then bear right to follow a steep, closed corner. Traverse right across

Pitch 2, near Pointe d'Aragon (5a).

OSSAU VALLEY

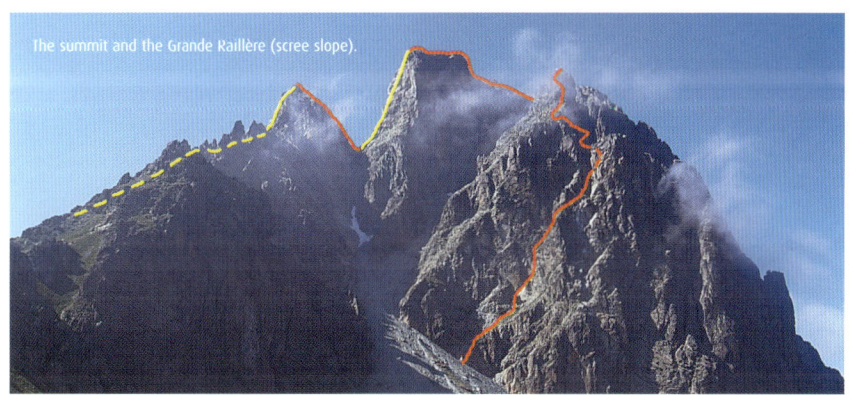

The summit and the Grande Raillère (scree slope).

The distinctive rock of the Pic du Midi.

PIC DU MIDI D'OSSAU
TRAVERSE OF THE FOUR PEAKS

OSSAU VALLEY

hanging slabs (30m, IV+). Move back into the middle of the gully and go up it to a belay just before a large, overhanging chimney (45m, II/III). Traverse right across a smooth wall, then climb stepped ledges and an area of more fractured rock to get to a belay below a steep wall (45m, IV). Traverse easily right along a ledge to an easy gully that is climbed to the foot of a steep wall (II+). Go up diagonally leftwards, climbing several short walls to regain the gully and then the notch at the foot of Pointe J. Santé (III). Climb to the summit (III), then come back to the notch.

To get to Pointe d'Aragon, climb a steep, 15m-high wall, then traverse right along a ledge to the foot of a corner (35m, IV). Climb the corner to ledges (40m, V-). Follow these ledges rightwards for about 80m, then head back left across light-coloured rock (II, do not go up too far) to the southern terraces on Pointe d'Aragon. Go up easy ground to the foot of the final step. Gain the summit by climbing either the crack on the right (IV) or the superb leaning crack on the left (V+).

Head north and go down a couloir for 20m, then traverse left across cracked slabs (III) to the crest of the ridge. Move on to its south-west side and traverse horizontally across easy ground to the ridge crest. Scramble easily down the ridge to the Brèche d'Aragon. Climb a wall on the right, then follow a chimney to the top of a steep step (III+). Go across easy ground towards a pointed block at the foot of a wall. Climb this wall (III) and the crack above to get to a flat summit.

Descend into the next notch (III), at the foot of a smooth wall. Traverse right along a large ledge to a crack to the right of some huge blocks. Climb the bottom part of this crack, then traverse right to the ridge. A steep wall (IV) leads to the top of the Rein de Pombie and the normal route to the Grand Pic.

From the top of the Grand Pic, descend easily south-westwards to a couloir. Climb down this couloir (III), then traverse diagonally left to a shoulder above a steep section (II). Head to its right-hand end and descend a steep chimney (III+). Continue down loose rock to the fork. Go up easy benches to a vertical step (II). Climb a wall (IV), then continue easily to the Petit Pic.

DESCENT

Head south down slabs and shattered rock to a large ledge above a steep section. Descend this section via two abseils (40m and 25m). Go back up the right bank for 5m to move on to the west face. Follow the cairns down the ridge, then climb down slabs on the Grande Raillère side to a horizontal section. Go down a grassy couloir for 200m, then go through the notch on the left, marked by a cairn and an old bicycle wheel! Follow the cairns across the ledges (II) to the Col de Peyreget path.

Looking down to the hut from Pointe d'Aragon.

HUTS AND INFORMATION

MOUNTAIN HUTS AND SHELTERS IN THE PYRENEES
www.pyrenees-pireneus.com and www.agrepy.org

MARIALLES HUT (1,700M) – FRANCE
Tel: 0033 468055799
www.refugedemarialles.fr
Open all year round but advance booking essential from 15 November to 15 May.
Route: Go through Vernet-les-Bains to Casteil. Turn right in Casteil and follow signs to the Col de Jou and Marialles. The road ends at the Col de Jou. Continue along the track (in good condition, closed to motor vehicles in July and August), then take the first left and continue to Marialles.

LLUIS ESTASEN HUT (1,647M) – SPAIN
Tel: 0034 608315312   tinyurl.com/lluisestasen
Open all year.
Route: Via the Cadi tunnel, the village of Saldes and the Mirador de Gresolet. 15-minute walk from the Mirador.

RENCLUSE HUT (2,140M) – SPAIN
Tel: 0034 974344646   tinyurl.com/renclusehut
Open all year.
Route: Go through Benasque to the Hospital de Benasque, from where a road (restricted access in summer) leads to the car park at La Besurta. Head south along the path to the hut (45 mins).

MAUPAS HUT (2,450M) – FRANCE
Tel: 0033 561988247   www.refugedumaupas.ffcam.fr
Staffed from mid-June to mid-September.
Route: From Luchon, head towards Superbagnères. Turn left before the resort to get to the car park at the end of the Lys Valley. Go over the bridge and follow the signposted path past L'Artigue, La Coume and Prat-long (3 hrs).

ESPINGO HUT (1,967M) – FRANCE
Tel: 0033 561792001   www.refugedespingo.ffcam.fr
Staffed from mid-May to mid-October.
Route: From Luchon, head towards the Col de Peyresourde. Turn left in the village of Castillon and go through Oô to the car park at Les Granges d'Astau. Continue along the path to Lac d'Oô and Lac d'Espingo (2 hrs).

PORTILLON HUT (2,571M) – FRANCE
Tel: 0033 561793815   www.refugeduportillon.ffcam.fr
Staffed from mid-May to October.
Route: From the Espingo hut, head south along the paved track beside Lac du Saussat, then continue along a good track to Portillon reservoir. The hut is at the western end of the dam (4 hrs).

ANGEL ORUS HUT (2,150M) – SPAIN
Tel: 0034 974344044   www.refugioangelorus.com
Staffed all year.
Route: Go through the village of Ériste (3km before Benasque). Immediately after the village, beside the generating station, turn left on to a narrow road. Go up the hairpins and continue to the car park at the end of the track. Follow the good path up the right bank of the valley to the hut (1½ hrs).

GLÈRE HUT (2,153M) – FRANCE
Tel: 0033 680012564   www.refugedelaglere.ffcam.fr
Staffed from mid-February to September.
Route: From Lourdes, go through Argelès-Gazost, Luz-Saint-Sauveur and Barèges (signs to Col du Tourmalet). After Barèges but before the car park at Tournaboup, turn right towards the auberge Chez Louisette and the Lienz Plateau. Go past the auberge and continue along the forest track to the funicular. Turn hard left and continue to the end of the valley. Park at 'Les Deux Tonnes' (small parking area), at the end of the valley, and continue on foot (1½ hrs).

ESTAUBÉ BIVOUAC SITE (2,100M) – FRANCE
Below the east face of the Astazou.
Route: Go across the Gloriettes dam (1,668m), then head due south along the path to the Hourquette d'Alans. At around 2,170m, below the Hourquette, a path traverses left towards the Brèche de Tuquerouye. An area of flat ground beside this path provides an excellent bivouac site; however, this area is inside the national park, so you will have to take your tent down first thing in the morning.

ESPUGUETTES HUT (2,030M) – FRANCE
Tel: 0033 562924063
www.refuge-des-espuguettes.blogspot.co.uk
Open from mid-June to mid-September.
Route: From Gavarnie, follow the path on the right bank of the stream towards the cirque, then turn left on to a path that starts beside a solitary building. Follow this path to the hut (1¾ hrs).

SARRADETS HUT (2,587M) – FRANCE
Tel: 0033 683381324   www.refugebrechederoland.ffcam.fr
Staffed from early June to September.
Route: From Gavarnie, follow the road through the resort of Espécières to the Col des Tentes. Continue on foot to the Col de Boucharo, then turn left on to the good path that leads to the hut (1½ hrs).

GORIZ HUT (2,200M) – SPAIN
Tel: 0034 974341201   www.goriz.es
Open all year.
Route: Drive through Torla to the car park at La Pradera (road closed to all traffic except buses in summer). Head east along the GR11 footpath to the hut (4 hrs).
The hut can also be reached from the village of Nerin via the track to the Cuello Arenas. This track is also closed to all traffic except buses in summer. It is 2 hrs from the Cuello Arenas to the hut.

TUQUEROUYE HUT (2,666M) – FRANCE/SPAIN BORDER
www.refugetuquerouye.ffcam.fr
Not staffed. Open all year. At the Brèche de Tuquerouye.
Route: Just after Gèdre, on the Gavarnie road, turn left on to the road to Lac des Gloriettes. Park just before the dam (1,668m). Go up the Estaubé Valley. Turn off the H.R.P. (Pyrenees High-Level Route) below the Hourquette d'Alans and follow the path southwards to climb the steep gully below the Brèche de Tuquerouye. This gully holds the snow until late in the season and crampons are often needed. The hut, which sleeps twelve, has become much more popular since it was renovated in 2003 (3½ hrs).

TUQUEROUYE BIVOUAC SITE (2,600M) – SPAIN
The tiny Tuquerouye hut is often full at weekends and during the summer, especially on rainy nights. A good alternative is to bivouac a little lower, beside the lake on the Spanish side of the Brèche. The boulderfield slightly lower contains a few excellent shelter stones. From the Pineta Valley, follow the good path towards the Balcon de Pineta (4 hrs).

OULETTES HUT (2,151M) – FRANCE
Tel: 0033 562926297   www.refugeoulettesdegaube.ffcam.fr
Staffed from late February to early October.
Route: From Cauterets, follow the road to Pont d'Espagne (paid car park). Go below the porch and follow the road, then take the path on the left (signpost) to Lac de Gaube
You can also use the chairlift. Continue south from the lake to the hut (2½ hrs).

BAYSSELANCE HUT (2,651M) – FRANCE
Tel: 0033 974776652   www.refugebayssellance.ffcam.fr
Staffed from 1 May to 30 September.
Route: From the Oulettes Hut, follow the GR10 south-east over the Hourquette d'Ossoue to the hut (4½ hrs). From Gavarnie, park at the Ossoue dam (1834m), then head north-west past the reservoir to the hut (2¾ hrs).

LARRIBET HUT (2,070M) – FRANCE
Tel: 0033 562972539   www.refugedelarribet.ffcam.fr
Staffed from late May to late September.
Route: From Argelès, go through Arrens and continue to the car park at the 'Maison du Parc' (1,470m). Head due south beside the stream, then turn right to follow the Larribet stream to the hut (2–2½ hrs).

ARRÉMOULIT HUT (2,305M)
Tel: 0033 559053179   www.arremoulit.fr
Staffed from early June to late September.
Route: From Pau, take the Oloron-Sainte-Marie road (N134) to Gan, then follow the D934 through Arudy and continue towards the Col du Pourtalet. Park at Le Caillou de Soques (1,400m), a few kilometres before the Col du Pourtalet. Head due east past the Cabane d'Arrious to the Col d'Arrious. Turn off the H.R.P. and head south-east past the steep Passage d'Orteig to the hut (3–3½ hrs). Another option is to take the Sagette gondola lift and then the tourist train from the resort of Artouste. The hut is 1 hr from the end of the railway.

POMBIE HUT (2,032M)
Tel: 0033 559053178   www.refugedepombie.ffcam.fr
Staffed from early June to mid-October.
Route: At the foot of the south face of the Pic du Midi d'Ossau. Park at Anéou (1,710m), just below the Col du Pourtalet. Head north and go over the Col de Soum de Pombie to get to the hut (1½ hrs). You can also start at Le Caillou de Soques (1,400m) and follow the H.R.P. (2½ hrs).

WEATHER
FRANCE
Tel: 08997102 + n° of the *département*
www.meteofrance.com   www.meteoblue.com

CATALONIA
Tel: 0034 934445000   www.meteo.cat

ARAGON
Tel: 0034 976596700   www.meteozgz.com

RESCUE
International emergency number: 112 or 18 (France).

FRANCE
Pyrénées Orientales: PGHM: 0033 468045103/CRS: 0033 468303057
Ariège: 0033 561642258
Haute-Garonne: 0033 561792836
Hautes-Pyrénées: 0033 562924141
Pyrénées-Atlantiques: 0033 559100250

SPAIN
Catalonia: 085
Val d'Aran: 0034 973640080
Guardia Civil mountain rescue: 062
Bénasque: 0034 974551008
Bielsa: 0034 974501025
Canfranc: 0034 974373066
Torla: 0034 974486160

Radio frequencies in Spain: ask at the huts.

FURTHER READING
Les Pyrénées: les 100 plus belles courses et randonnées, Patrice de Bellefon (Denoël, 1989)
Passages Pyrénéens, R. Munch, C. Ravier, R. Thivel (les topos du Pin à Crochets, 1999)
La vie des hommes de la montagne dans les Pyrénées, racontée par la toponymie: Marcellin Bérot (Éditions Milan, 2002)
Souvenirs d'un montagnard, Henry Russell
L'aventure du Balaïtous, Jean-François Labourie (Rando editions, 1993)
La Dent d'Orlu, Jean-Denis Achard (J'idée edition, 2002)
Les Pyrénées en face, Laurent Lafforgue (Version Originale, 2006)
Crestas del Pirineo: II Cataluña y Andorra, Pedro Lopez Gonzalez (Barrabes, 2005)

The routes included in this guidebook are presented for information only. Every mountaineer is responsible for his or her own decisions. Choices must take into account one's abilities and the risks arising from the conditions in the mountains. The route descriptions are accurate for the conditions and date on which they were climbed; however, climbers should check that a chosen route has not changed in any way, for example, due to rockfall, glacial retreat or removal of *in situ* gear. The authors, editors and publishers cannot be held responsible for any accidents that occur on any of the routes described in this guidebook. As the guidebook is not updated at frequent intervals, it cannot be considered expert testimony in a court of law.

SAFETY STATEMENT
Climbing and mountaineering are activities that carry a risk of personal injury or death. Participants must be aware of and accept that these risks are present and they should be responsible for their own actions and involvement. Nobody involved in the writing and production of this guidebook accepts any responsibility for any errors that it contains, nor are they liable for any injuries or damage that may arise from its use. Climbing and mountaineering are inherently dangerous and the fact that individual descriptions in this volume do not point out such dangers does not mean that they do not exist. Take care.